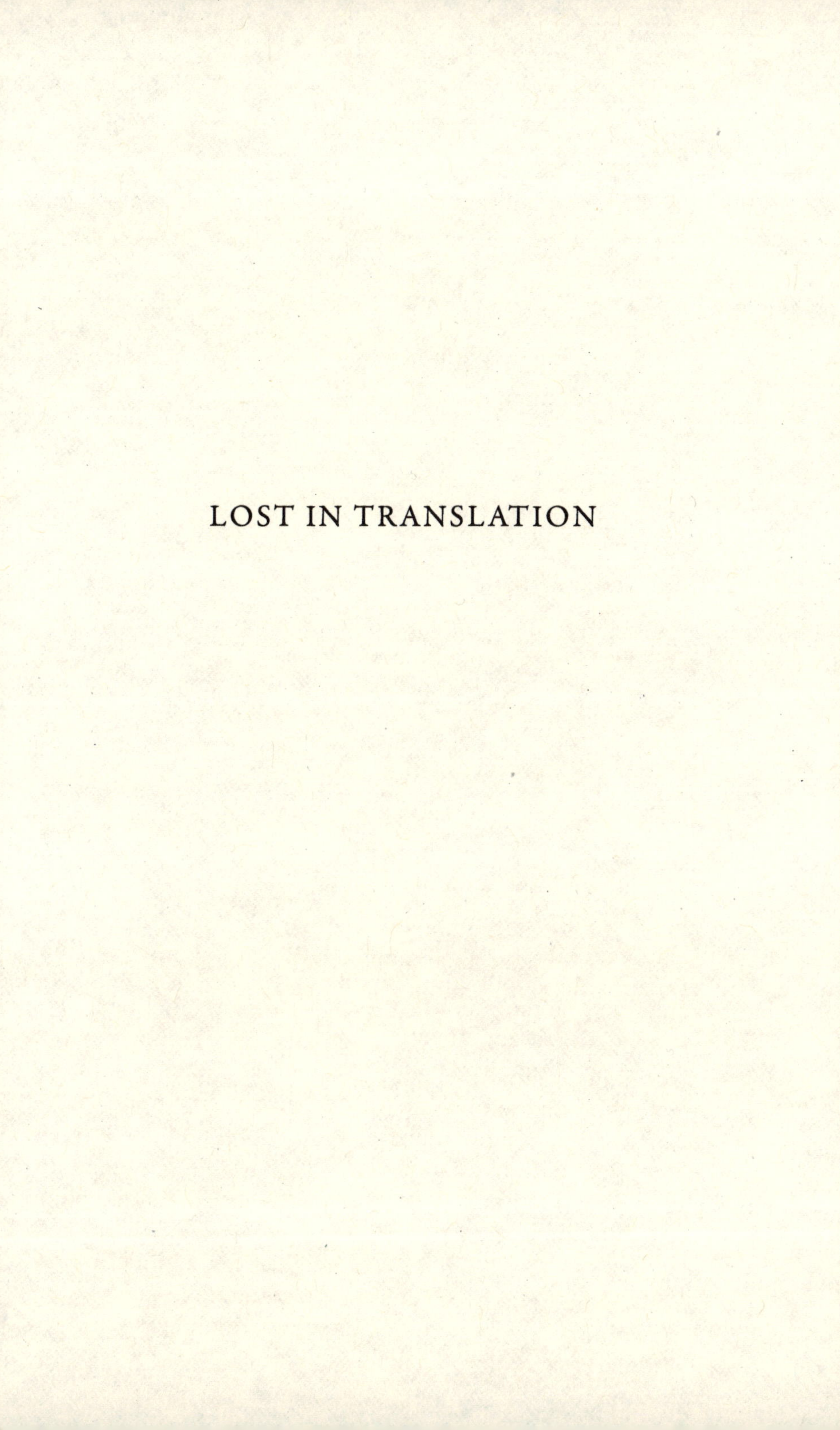

LOST IN TRANSLATION

LOST IN TRANSLATION

RECOVERING THE ORIGINS OF FAMILIAR BIBLICAL WORDS

JOEL S. BADEN

FORTRESS PRESS
Minneapolis

LOST IN TRANSLATION
Recovering the Origins of Familiar Biblical Words

30 29 28 27 26 25 2 3 4 5 6 7 8 9 10

Library of Congress Control Number: 2024055043 (print)

Cover image: Hebrew letter in watercolor, from iStock
Cover design: Laurie Ingram Art + Design.com

Print ISBN: 978-1-5064-9710-5
eBook ISBN: 978-1-5064-9711-2

For Sara,
whose idea this book evidently was,
with all my love

CONTENTS

II
Words Connected to People

Intermezzo

III
Words That Connect God and People

Intermezzo

Postscript

ACKNOWLEDGMENTS

My thanks go first to my wife Sara—whose idea this book evidently was—and to the other friends, colleagues, and family members who, in conversations about this project, suggested many of the words that are now included in these essays.

I am grateful to Carey Newman, who kindly but firmly guided this book from proposal to publication and who helped me understand what it was I was really doing here.

This book really found its footing through conversation and collaboration with Helena Martin, my student, colleague, and friend. I am lucky to know and work with her, and I am thankful for all the advice and guidance she gave me on how to write these essays.

Of course, nothing is possible without the support and love of my family: Sara first and foremost; our children Zara and Iris and Avery and Toby; and my parents.

Introduction

FOR MOST READERS of the Bible—at least in America—modern English translations, usually without substantial accompanying notes, are the primary means to access the text. Translations are a wonderful thing: they allow access to the Bible for those who aren't able to read ancient Hebrew (or Greek, or Latin)—which is to say, most people. They also provide a sense of ease: this language is my language; these words are my words; their meanings are simple and transparent; they have been translated not only into my language but into my cultural idiom.

And yet—our cultural idiom isn't that of the ancient Israelite world that produced the Bible. And the words that we read in English, though seemingly transparent to us, do not actually let us see through the thousands of years back to the original Hebrew in which the text was written. The words that we think we understand today are often quite different from the ones that they're ostensibly representing. This isn't due to faulty translation but to the very nature of translation itself. We are more distant from the original Hebrew than we realize.

There are a variety of ways that the original meanings of biblical words have been lost or obscured. Sometimes this loss of original meaning is due to a perfectly natural process of linguistic change. Over time, in every language, words take on new meanings and shed older ones, such that the same word might end up communicating something quite different from what it once did. For the Bible, this process has happened multiple times. The Hebrew of the earliest biblical texts and that of the latest are as distant as our modern English is from that of Chaucer. The disappearance of virtually all the ancient Near Eastern cultures and their languages already at the turn of the Common Era meant that it was impossible, until the last two hundred years, to understand a slew of biblical words. Even the rabbis of the first centuries CE didn't know what plenty of Hebrew words meant. And then again fifteen hundred years later, the King James Version (KJV) set the standard for English Bible translations. But here we are five hundred years after that, and the language of the KJV is different from our own. The linguistic gap between us and the original Hebrew of the Bible is therefore both multi-millennial and multilingual. It's not a small leap—it's the Grand Canyon.

Then there is the very act of translation itself. The best translations may attempt to render the original text as accurately as possible, but all translation is interpretation. A word in Biblical Hebrew may not have a single perfect parallel in English. It may correlate to multiple English words—the ancient Hebrew lexicon is much smaller than that of modern English—or maybe to none at all. A translator is faced with a difficult, sometimes impossible, task.

That difficulty is compounded by the question of whether to give preference to the original text or the target language. With the Bible, this question is especially acute. For while the Hebrew Bible is two to three thousand years old, its readers, generally speaking, expect it to speak to them today, to be constantly relevant. Hew too closely to the Hebrew and to the ancient world from which it emerged, and a translator risks creating a text that is—for the Bible—too weird, too distant. But lean too far to our own linguistic and cultural expectations, and the Bible ends up feeling almost overly familiar: it merely reinforces our own sensibilities.

The common, almost universal, tendency is to assume that the world we're reading about isn't all that different from our own. If you've ever seen the wonderful, illustrated Bibles from medieval France, say, or from early modern Germany, you may have noted that the characters are all depicted wearing clothing from medieval France or from early modern Germany. The architecture of the buildings is imagined to be the same, the weapons are the same, and so on. It may seem amusing to us now, but in fact we do the same thing with the very language of the Bible. We see a word in English and assume that it meant the same thing to ancient audiences then as it does to us now. But words have meaning only within cultural systems. If our culture is different from theirs—and it is—then even the same word will resonate quite differently.

And, finally, there is the theological overlay that comes from thousands of years of specifically (though not exclusively) Christian tradition. Biblical terms have been taken up and transformed into major theological concepts—sometimes even into doctrines. For a reader who knows the Bible only as a Christian text—and that's many, if not most, readers—some words will inevitably echo with the big, weighty meaning that their faith has attached to them. This is familiarizing for the reader—"Hey, look, it's a concept that we know and care about!"—but also ends up pushing the world of the text itself, the world of ancient Israel, even farther away. Such distancing happens in many ways, but one of the most common is the trend toward abstracted or spiritualized understandings of words that once had tangible, mundane, embodied meanings and uses. The theologizing of the ancient Israelite literature that makes up the Hebrew Bible meant lifting it, and the words that constitute it, out of the real world and day-to-day life from which it emerged. Once the Bible was taken to mean something more than what it says on its surface, the realities that lay behind it—the human bodies, the politics, the economics, and so on—were soon forgotten.

This book is meant as an attempt to undo some of the phenomena just described. It is not a corrective, per se. That is, I don't at all think that modern English understandings of the text are necessarily wrong just because they are the result of linguistic change, or translational choice, or theological interpretation. I don't think that the original meaning of the text is the only true one, or that it should be determinative for how anyone engages with the Bible today. That said, I also realize that for many people who take the Bible seriously, be they clergy or laity, what it originally said and meant is important, perhaps supremely important. And so this book is meant not as a corrective but as a supplement of sorts.

We need not give up the ways that we understand the text today. But we might expand them somewhat, first by recognizing that they aren't identical to the text's original meaning, and then by, perhaps, trying to integrate what a word means now with what it meant then. Words are not flat or univocal. They can carry multiple meanings, multiple nuances, multiple echoes. A deeper understanding of them doesn't challenge our reading of the text; it only enhances it.

This book is not a sustained argument so much as it is an iterative one. Each of the short essays that follows explores a single word from the English Bible, a word that is relatively common or familiar or theologically important. I try to show that how the word is usually understood today is different from how it would have been understood by the Bible's authors and original audience and to illuminate the insights we might gain from bringing those two meanings into conversation. I have also organized the words by broad theme: words about God, words about people, and words about the relationship between God and people. (And a few that are about language itself, in a way.) For ease of cross-reference, when a word that appears in one essay has its own essay, it appears in *italics*. Taken together, it is my hope that this book will help the reader realize that the words of the Bible are never static, but are always changing, shaped by (and shaping) the cultures in which they are read.

I

Words Connected to God

§ 1

The Lord (יהוה, *adonai* or *yahweh*)

Thus shall you say to the Israelites: The Lord, the God of your ancestors, the God of Abraham, the God of Isaac, and the God of Jacob, has sent me to you.

Exodus 3:15 (NRSV)

WHAT'S IN A name? For most readers of the Bible, it's a moot question, because there is no name here. "The Lord" is a title, equivalent to "God," or "the Almighty." This is a translation with a long history, as ancient as anything in the Bible—but it does the reader a real disservice.

The name of Israel's deity was יהוה, probably, according to virtually all scholars, to be pronounced "Yahweh." Not a title—a proper name. There's nothing surprising about this: Every ancient deity had a proper name. Marduk, Osiris, and Zeus are all familiar to us. The nations surrounding Israel each had their own national deity: Chemosh for the Moabites, Milcom for the Ammonites, Qos for the Edomites. The Canaanite pantheon was led by El and Baal—two proper names that came to be used for the common nouns "god" and "lord" in Hebrew. And Israel's god was named Yahweh.

In the ancient world, and particularly in Israel, the name of the deity was more than just a name. It was itself a manifestation of the deity—it contained and wielded power, it was an extension of the divine being. The prohibition in the Ten Commandments against "taking the name of the Lord in vain" is a reflection of this concept. To say the deity's name was to invoke his presence (and I should note that here and elsewhere I use the masculine pronoun when referring to Israel's god—though we may think of God as ungendered, in Israel, and in the texts it produced, Yahweh, the national deity, was decidedly male). Even God takes oaths by his own name: "I swear by my great name," says Yahweh in Jeremiah 44:26. Misuse of the divine name was equivalent to the misuse of the *sacred* objects in the temple. Vows that used the name of the deity were powerful, and to break one was to trespass against Yahweh himself. We still have a version of this in the courtroom: swearing on the Bible with the phrase "so help me God" invokes that same power and the same fear of divine punishment.

It was the very power of the divine name that led to its being translated virtually out of existence. The first step, however, was probably not translation but pronunciation. Those who read the text aloud in Hebrew, early Jews, instilled the tradition of seeing the name יהוה but pronouncing it *adonai*—that is, the Hebrew word for "lord." It has been pronounced that way in Jewish contexts for over two millennia, with the understanding that the proper name, referred to sometimes as "the Tetragrammaton" or "the four letters"—YHWH—should never be spoken aloud. The earliest translation of the Hebrew Bible, the Greek version from roughly the third century BCE known as the Septuagint, followed this reading tradition by rendering יהוה as *kyrios* or "lord." And so has virtually every translation ever since.

As something of an aside, in the tenth to eleventh century CE, Jewish scribes began to add vowels to the biblical text, which previously contained only the consonants, in order to ensure consistent pronunciation. When they vocalized the divine name, they put in the vowels of the word that was actually spoken rather than what was written. So the consonants יהוה received the vowels from *adonai*. Christians in the

Middle Ages, unclear as to what was going on, mistakenly transliterated the divine name with the alternative vowels. The result was the now-common form "Jehovah"—which is not, and never was, the name of Israel's deity.

The translation of יהוה as "the Lord" is, in a positive sense, a longstanding gesture of respect for Jewish tradition. On the other hand, something fundamentally important has been lost. From a historical perspective, the substitution of "the Lord" for "Yahweh" obscures the religious context in which the Bible was written. "The Lord" is a singular deity—there can be only one. It is a universal sort of title. "Yahweh," by contrast, is particular: it is the name of Israel's deity specifically, in contrast to the other deities who existed in the same time and general vicinity (Chemosh, Milcom, Qos, El, Baal, etc.). When we read in the Shema, in Deuteronomy 6:4, "Hear O Israel, the Lord is our god, the Lord alone," the verse resounds with monotheism. But if we read it instead as "Hear O Israel, Yahweh is our god, Yahweh alone," it rings differently—not as the recognition of the sole deity, but as the selection of one deity out of many.

Sometimes the translation of יהוה as "the Lord" results in some strange moments. In the Bible, non-Israelites refer to Israel's deity by name. In Genesis 26, the Philistine Abimelech says to Isaac, "We see plainly that יהוה has been with you" (Gen 26:28). If we translate "the Lord" here, we end up with a non-Israelite referring to a foreign (to him) deity as "the Lord." When we read it as a proper name, however, it makes all the sense in the world: "Yahweh, your deity—but not ours—has been with you." Or, in the epigraph above, Moses asks, "When I come to the Israelites and they ask me 'What is the name of the deity who sent you,' what shall I say to them?" The answer isn't "the Lord"—it's "Yahweh." Yet every translation reads "the Lord" there, despite it being a rather nonsensical, or at least unsatisfying, response.

In our modern (and two-millennia-old) monotheistic context, "the Lord" is a translation that speaks to what we have come to believe about the nature of God. It is therefore not "wrong"—but it's also not entirely right. Or, at least, in its desire to be universal, it is ironically incomplete, losing the sense of specificity that a proper name conveys. Here the Hebrew reader has the advantage; though one may say aloud the equivalent of "the Lord," what one sees on the page is still the unambiguous four-letter proper name. A conscious choice is made every time the name is encountered. If English readers were also aware of that choice, aware of the binary of universality and specificity that lies behind "the Lord," it would make their experience of the text considerably richer.

§ 2

Holy/Sacred (קדוש, *qadosh*)

You shall be holy, for I the Lord your God am holy.

Leviticus 19:2 (NRSV)

HOLINESS IN THE Hebrew Bible is, as today, a quality associated with the divine sphere. Isaiah often refers to God simply as "the holy one," or "the holy one of Israel." Things, people, places, and even times that belong to the deity are given this label. Animals are naturally profane—until they have been designated as a sacrificial offering, at which point they become holy. The cultic objects in the sanctuary—the table, the lampstand, the altar, the basin, etc.—are holy. Aaron is just a normal person until he is anointed to serve as priest, at which point he too becomes holy. The Tabernacle, the Temple, and Mount Zion, are all called holy, for they are where the deity resides. The *Sabbath* and the festival days are holy times. God's name, Yahweh, is holy.

Strange, then, for Yahweh to call on all of Israel to be holy, as in Leviticus 19:2. Except in an eschatological utopia, as imagined in Isaiah 61:5–6, for example, not all Israelites will be priests, the biblical category of holy people. This use of קדוש is clarified, however, when the word is read with its primary meaning in mind: "separate," "distinct."

That which is holy is set apart from that which is "normal." There are innumerable animals, objects, people, places, times, and names that have no special designation; those that belong to God are distinctive, though they may look exactly the same. And while "holy" may have come to be used almost exclusively with reference to the divine, there are places where it retains a seemingly non-divine meaning. If, according to Deuteronomy 22:9, you sow your vineyard with a second kind of seed, the yield from the vineyard becomes קדוש—"set aside," "unusable."

This sense of prohibition on normal use is common across many examples of holiness. A holy animal can only be sacrificed; it cannot be used domestically. A priest cannot own land; no work may be done on the *Sabbath*; God's name cannot be used inappropriately. Yet these represent a second conceptual stage. First a thing is set apart; then regulations are instituted to maintain that separation.

The *Sabbath* is a wonderful example of this phenomenon, even within the biblical account itself. At creation, of course, God declares the seventh day holy, because on that day God ceases from the work of creation (Gen 2:3). The day is distinctive: It is not like the previous six days. Yet God's declaration of its holiness carries no practical implications, at least not yet. It is just marked unlike the other days of the week. Only later, when Israel, alone among the nations, has received the laws of the *Sabbath*, is the holiness of the day put into practice in any way. In the Ten Commandments, we first read, as we knew, that the *Sabbath* is holy (Exod 20:8); this general statement is followed by instructions as to how to behave so as to mark that holiness (Exod 20:9–10). We find the same pattern a bit further on: the *Sabbath* is holy (Exod 31:14); what that means in practical terms is that you may not work on it (31:15).

What does it mean, then, for Israel to be holy? It means that they are to be distinctive from all other peoples by following these laws, the divine instructions that are meant only for them: "You must keep my sabbaths, that you may know that I the Lord have consecrated you" (Exod 31:13, JPS). Israel has been chosen among all the nations to be God's people; they must act differently from everyone else. It is no coincidence that the central statement of this idea, in Leviticus 19:2, comes immediately after a set of laws explicitly described as a means of differentiating Israel from the Canaanites and the Egyptians (Leviticus 18).

This is the meaning, too, of the famous line in Exodus 19:6: "You shall be to me a kingdom of priests and a holy nation." It is not that all Israelites are to actually become priests. Rather, just as the priests are distinctive within Israel, so Israel should be distinctive among the nations, by keeping the *covenant*, the laws given to Israel alone.

As for God's holiness, it, too, is, at its root, about distinctiveness: "Who is like you, O Yahweh, among the divine beings? Who is like you, majestic in holiness?" (Exod 15:11). Yahweh, Israel's god, is not like the other deities out there. Yahweh cares more for his people (Deut 4:7), gives wiser laws (Deut 4:8), and is more powerful (Deut 4:34). As monotheism gained traction in the Bible, the notion of holiness was transformed into one not of distinctiveness from other deities but of distinctiveness from the mundane world as a whole: God is simply "other" in a qualitative sense.

Yet for much of the Bible, we might understand holiness as representing something of an anxiety of identity. Israel was but one nation among many and a relatively small and insignificant one at that. They understood themselves to be special because their deity was special; because they, in upholding the unique laws of their god, marked themselves as different. In this understanding, Israel was, most likely, in fact not special at all: What nation wouldn't say the same of itself? Yet this sense of distinctiveness, expressed primarily through observance of distinct practices, lies at the root of Israel's, and Judaism's, survival down through the millennia.

§ 3

Glory (כבוד, *kavod*)

The cloud covered the tent of meeting, and the glory of the Lord filled the Tabernacle.

Exodus 40:34 (NRSV)

"Glory" is a pretty nebulous term in English. It has to do with honor, renown, praise, exaltation—it's definitely a good thing, but it's intangible and hard to define. The Biblical Hebrew equivalent, כבוד, shares some of these qualities. It can mean "honor," in the sense of the respect due to a king or deity. It isn't far from "renown," as in the great reputation of God in Israel and among the nations. But in the Bible, the word can also—and, in fact, very frequently does—have a much more tangible meaning.

The root of כבוד means "heavy." Two common uses of the word pick up on this weightiness, one pertaining mostly to humans and one pertaining to God. The first of these uses of "glory" is as an equivalent or parallel to "wealth." "Do not be afraid when some become rich, when the wealth [כבוד] of their houses increases," the psalmist writes. "For when they die they will carry nothing away; their wealth [כבוד] will not go down after them" (Ps 49:16–17, NRSV). Here there is almost a direct contrast with glory in the sense of "honor," which one does indeed retain even after death.

When Balaam refuses to curse Israel, Balak says to him, "I said 'I will reward you richly,' but the Lord has denied you any reward" (Num 24:11, NRSV). The words "reward" (both times) and "richly" in this translation are renderings of כבוד or its verbal equivalent. Similarly, Laban's sons complain that Jacob has "gained all this wealth"—כבוד—"from what belonged to our father" (Gen 31:1, NRSV). Isaiah prophesies that in the eschatological time when all the nations come to worship Israel's god, "you [Israel] shall enjoy the wealth of nations, and revel in their riches [כבוד]" (Isa 61:6, JPS).

This use of כבוד feels rather modern: After all, it remains the case that wealth is one of the dominant markers of social status. In the ancient world, when wealth disparity was even more stark than it is today and when the "heavy" wealth—gold and silver—was available almost exclusively to the extraordinarily elite, it was sensible for wealth and weight, כבוד, to be aligned with honor and glory. Perhaps less obvious, though also modern in its way, is the extension of this sense of wealth to the divine realm in the form of tribute. The prophet Haggai complains that the rebuilt Temple is a pale imitation of the original: "Who is left among you that saw this house in its former glory [כבוד]? . . . I will shake all the nations, so that the treasure of all nations shall come, and I will fill this house with splendor [כבוד]" (Hag 2:3, 7, NRSV). Glory may be an intangible quality, but it is demonstrated through very tangible means.

More conceptually distant from our modern sensibilities is the frequent use of "glory" to refer not to an abstract quality but to the very real presence of God. God and God's "glory" are often identical: "The Lord is high above all nations, and his glory above the heavens" (Ps 113:4, NRSV). This is most clear in the Tabernacle. This most *sacred* space is filled not with some quality of the deity, but with the deity himself: "There I will meet with you, and there I will speak with you. . . .

I will abide among the Israelites" (Exod 29:42, 45, JPS). When the "glory of the Lord" fills the Tabernacle, that is Yahweh literally taking up residence. When the Tabernacle is established, and the sacrificial rites inaugurated, "the glory of the Lord appeared to all the people" (Lev 9:23, NRSV)—not a quality of the deity, but the deity himself. Admittedly, what the people see of God isn't a human form: "The appearance of the glory of the Lord was like a devouring fire," as we read in Exodus 24:17 (NRSV). But the very idea that the glory of the Lord has any appearance at all testifies to its physical reality.

The name "Ichabod" is another reminder of this tangible divine glory. The "chabod" part of the name is our word, כבוד. The prefix, "I," indicates absence of some sort. We read, "She named the child Ichabod, meaning, 'The glory has departed from Israel,' because the ark of God had been captured" (1 Sam 4:21, NRSV). The physical departure of the *ark*, the divine throne and marker of God's presence, is equated with the departure of God's glory. Ezekiel is perhaps the most open about the physicality of the כבוד, describing it as having an appearance (Ezek 1:28), rising (3:12), standing (3:23), going up (10:4), going out (10:8), and coming (43:2). For the biblical authors in the priestly tradition—the P source of the Pentateuch and Ezekiel, most prominently—the "glory" of God is little more than a euphemism for Yahweh himself.

It is certainly true that "glory" can be a mere quality in the Bible. "Sing the glory of his name, give to him glorious praise," as in Psalm 66:2 (NRSV). But just as our modern idea of a totally invisible, intangible, omnipresent deity is foreign to the Hebrew Bible, so, too, is the idea of a totally abstract "glory." When we read "glory" as an ephemeral quality of the deity (or of humans, for that matter), we lose some of the depth, the tangibility, the weightiness, of the ancient world and worldview. What is mere idea for us was very real, very present, for the ancient authors and audiences of the Bible.

§ 4

Angel (מלאך, *mal'akh*)

An angel of the Lord appeared to him in a blazing fire out of a bush.
Exodus 3:2 (JPS)

Any good reader of Milton can tell you that angels are divine beings with distinctive and identifiable names and personalities. Some of them can, out of spite and envy, even rebel against God. But you'd be hard-pressed to find such angels in the Bible. Even Milton's Satan, though he appears in the Bible to be sure, is no rebel (see *Satan*)—and he's not even called an angel. In the book of Daniel, we meet Gabriel, who interprets visions for Daniel. Gabriel is also certainly not a rebel and is not endowed with much distinctive personality. And, though Gabriel is decidedly a divine being, he also is never referred to as an "angel."

As it turns out, although there are hundreds of references to "angels" in the Hebrew Bible, not a single one has a name or any personality traits to speak of. This is because, in the Bible, "angels" aren't angels. At least, not how we've come to think of them.

The Hebrew word commonly translated as "angel" is מלאך, which means, quite simply, "messenger." This is certainly an apt description of a standard angelic function. But it's also a very human function. And the word מלאך is used in the Bible not only for divine messengers but for human ones as well. Jacob sends messengers (מלאך) to Esau (Gen 32:4); Moses sends messengers (מלאך) to the king of Edom

(Num 20:14); Joshua, Gideon, Jephthah, Saul, David, and countless other characters send messengers (מלאך). It was a standard form of long-distance communication; written letters are exceedingly rare in the Bible. Our understanding of the divine מלאך should be grounded in its earthly counterpart—specifically, since Israel's god was understood as a heavenly king, in the royal messenger.

The messenger sent by a monarch fulfills two roles. There is the communicative: the passing on of words (greetings, promises, threats) from the king. And there is the representative: the messenger effectively standing in for the body of the king in absentia. How the king's emissary is treated is an indication of respect, or lack thereof, toward the king himself. For example, when the messengers David sends to the Ammonites have their beards shaved and garments torn, it provokes a war (2 Sam 10:1–7).

So, too, the divine messenger. Words from God are delivered to humans, of course, from Hagar (the first human to encounter a divine מלאך) to Haggai, a human prophet given the title "מלאך of Yahweh" (Hag 1:13). But just as importantly, God's מלאך represents the deity, speaking for and often in the very voice of God. "I brought you up from Egypt and I took you into the land which I had promised on oath to your fathers," says not God but a מלאך of Yahweh to the Israelites (Judg 2:1, NRSV).

We can even go further: God's מלאך is, in the Bible, not just a representative but an extension of the deity. This may have been conceptually how royal human messengers were also understood, but, because God has a (for lack of a better term) mobility that humans don't have, this is not just conceptual extension but literal, physical extension. Thus a מלאך of Yahweh appears to Moses in the burning bush (Exod 3:2), but once Moses stops to investigate it is no longer a messenger but Yahweh himself who speaks (3:4–6). Going the other way, in Genesis 18 the narrator tells us that Yahweh appears to Abraham (18:1), but when we see the scene through Abraham's eyes he sees not the deity but simply three men (18:2). The messenger and the sender are indistinguishable; the מלאך and the deity are one and the same.

The Hebrew Bible is decidedly ambivalent about whether God can be seen. It is at least clear that seeing God is both terrifying and dangerous ("Man may not see me and live," [Exod 33:20, JPS]). The מלאך, however, is decidedly see-able (even if the experience is still a little scary, as Gideon realizes: "Alas, O Lord God! For I have seen a מלאך of Yahweh face to face!" [Judg 6:22, JPS]). Divine messengers walk with, talk with, even eat with humans (Gen 18:8). They are not lesser beings; rather, they are the embodied form of God.

How did the מלאך become the "angel" we know today? It's not a translation issue, not really: Our English word "angel" comes from the Greek word *angelos*, which is the translation of מלאך and which in Greek, as in Hebrew, also meant simply "messenger," human or divine. The shift began, it seems, in early Judaism, already exemplified in part by Gabriel in the book of Daniel. Angels began to be more than conduits of divine speech; they played the role of interpreter, showing visions to humans and explaining their meanings. With this new job description came not a new title, but rather new proper names. And once these figures had distinctive names, it wasn't long before they had distinctive character traits as well. The once-uniform מלאך—each, as nothing more than a manifestation of the deity, identical with the next—gave rise to an entire extended angelic universe.

Our modern understanding of angels might lead to reading personality traits back into and onto the biblical מלאך. This would, of course, obscure the nature of the מלאך as extension of the deity. On the other hand, we might also read the biblical function of the מלאך forward into the later concept of angels. What might Milton make of the idea that his Lucifer is, in the end, an embodied manifestation of the divine will?

§ 5

Satan (שטן, *satan*)

The Lord said to Satan, "Have you considered my servant Job?"
Job 1:8 (NRSV)

THE VERSE ABOVE is a terrific example of how tradition influences translation and of how traditional translations can obscure what's actually happening in the text. There are two figures in conversation here. One is identified, in this English translation, with a title: "The Lord"; the other, with a proper name: "Satan." Yet in the Hebrew, the situation is exactly reversed. What is translated here as "the Lord" is יהוה, the proper name of the Israelite god (see *Lord*). And, perhaps more surprisingly, what is translated here as "Satan" is השטן, "the adversary": not a name but a title.

For many, especially for Christians, Satan is a figure of pure malevolence, an enemy of God, a rebellious and fallen *angel*. The origins of this idea are quite ancient. While the notion of Satan as a fallen *angel* goes back to Origen and Jerome, the identification of Satan with the embodiment of evil is found even earlier, in the New Testament, in the book of Revelation: "The great dragon was thrown down, that ancient serpent, who is called the Devil and Satan, the deceiver of the whole world" (Rev 12:9, NRSV). "That ancient serpent," for whatever it's worth, doesn't refer to the snake in the garden of Eden, despite longstanding tradition identifying the snake with Satan. Satan doesn't show up in Genesis, not in Eden or anywhere else. "That ancient serpent" is almost certainly Leviathan, the great sea serpent defeated by God in one of the biblical creation myths.

In the Hebrew Bible, however, שטן isn't the name of the Devil. In its earliest usages, it's just the common noun for "adversary," or "opponent." The Philistines worry that David will be a שטן to them in battle (1 Sam 29:4). God raises one שטן after another to trouble the peaceful reign of Solomon: first Hadad the Edomite (1 Kgs 11:14), then Rezon (1 Kgs 11:23). These aren't devils or *angels*; they're just regular humans, and they are שטן only in relation to another human.

When שטן is used of a divine figure, it is not as God's adversary, but, much like Hadad and Rezon, as a divinely appointed adversary to a human. In the story of Balaam and his donkey, the divine messenger sent by God identifies himself as שטן: "The angel of the Lord said to him . . . 'I have come out as an adversary, because your way is perverse before me'" (Num 22:32, NRSV). Here the שטן figure is acting as an extension of God—as God's prosecutor, as it were. And this is precisely how שטן appears in Psalm 109: "Let an accuser (שטן) stand on his right. When he is tried, let him be found guilty" (Ps 109:6–7).

Satan's biggest role in the Hebrew Bible comes, however, in the book of Job, where he is responsible for all of Job's suffering. Yet even here he is not malevolent. He is simply trying to make a theological point: that even the best-behaved humans are loyal only because God allows them to live comfortably. Yes, he acts as a tempter, trying to get Job to curse God, but this is less character trait and more professional role. God may not agree with the שטן, but God is perfectly willing to engage with him and let him do his thing. Again, God is acting here as judge, and the שטן as prosecutor, making a case, bringing evidence.

The role of "the adversary" probably had its origins in the judicial sphere, as the prosecutor or accuser. It would come to be used more generally as "adversary," as with Solomon's political opponents. But toward the end of the Hebrew Bible, "the adversary" would come to be purely a tempter. In the earlier book of Samuel, God becomes angry at Israel: "and he incited David against them, saying, 'Go and number Israel and Judah'" (2 Sam 24:1, JPS). When this same episode is recounted in the later book of Chronicles, however, it is no longer God who is responsible: "Satan stood up against Israel, and incited David to count the people of Israel" (1 Chr 21:1, NRSV). It perhaps only here that we see the first glimmers of what would come to be Satan's role and identity in later tradition. And even here, if we read the two versions of the story together, the Satan figure is still only doing exactly what God wanted done.

Many factors went into the transformation of the Hebrew Bible's neutral "adversary" into the later Christian embodiment of all evil: the rise of dualistic theologies, early Christian doctrines of sin, famous art and literature (Dante, Milton), and more. Notably, despite the trajectory of the Hebrew Bible and the prevalence in the Second Temple period of stories about the angelic world, including heavenly rebellions, Judaism never took up the idea of Satan as an identifiable evil counterpart to God. Which is to say, the nature—indeed, the very existence—of the Satan we know today wasn't obvious or inevitable. It was, rather, shaped by cultural factors of various types; it developed over time in order to serve particular interpretive or theological ends.

One may, of course, read the references to שטן in the Hebrew Bible as referring to the later Christian figure of Satan, just as one may read references to the "suffering servant" in Isaiah as referring to Jesus. But to lose entirely the original notion of "the adversary" is also to lose an important aspect of the Hebrew Bible's understanding of God. For the שטן (if not Satan) is not in opposition to God but is, rather, an extension of God. His arguments, prosecutions, and even temptations are divinely approved and often divinely ordained. Much of the shift from שטן to Satan might be attributed to an increasing discomfort with the notion that God could be responsible for anything other than the perfectly good. But that says more about us, perhaps, than it does about God, or about Satan.

§ 6

Cherub (כרוב, *keruv*)

> *He drove the man out, and stationed east of the garden of Eden the cherubim and the fiery ever-turning sword, to guard the way to the tree of life.*
>
> Genesis 3:24 (JPS)

OVER HALF A millennium ago, the great Italian painter Raphael gave us what has become the indelible image of cherubs: two chubby-faced little angels with wings, their eyes cast heavenward. Adorable, lovable, so cute they could hardly hurt a fly. And thus, about as far from what a cherub actually is—or at least was—as one could imagine.

The most extensive description in the Bible of a cherub comes from the book of Ezekiel. Though somewhat hard to picture, the details are basically this: four faces (ox, human, lion, and eagle); four wings, with human-like hands under each wing; a wheel, somehow; and, oh yes—covered all over with eyes (Ezek 10:8–22). To be fair, Ezekiel's vision of cherubs is probably idiosyncratic. But it should at least give us a sense of just how removed from the biblical notion the famous Renaissance paintings are.

Cherubs have come to be understood as a type of *angel*. But in fact they're never identified as such. *Angels*, at least in the Hebrew Bible, are messengers: Their purpose is to communicate on behalf of God. Cherubs, on the other hand, don't do any communicating whatsoever.

They are, rather, guardians, or gatekeepers. In their first, and perhaps most famous, occurrence in the Bible, they guard the way into the garden of Eden after Adam and Eve's expulsion (Gen 3:24). In Ezekiel, they drive the iniquitous out from the mountain of God (Ezek 28:16).

They are most common, however, in the descriptions of the *ark* inside the holy of holies, the dwelling place of God. There, two cherubs are said to sit above the *ark*, their wings outstretched toward each other, thereby creating a seat for the deity (Exod 25:22; 1 Kgs 8:7; 1 Chr 28:18)—hence the widespread, if not very common, title for God: "Yahweh who is enthroned on the cherubs" (1 Sam 4:4; 2 Sam 6:2; 2 Kgs 19:15; Isa 37:16; Ps 80:1; 99:1; 1 Chr 13:6). In 2 Samuel 22:11, God is described as a warrior riding on a cherub. None of these descriptions really sounds like the sort of stuff that a little baby would be doing. These are jobs for big, strong, maybe even scary creatures. Creatures like, say, giant hybrid animals—lions with wings, something like that. Something, in fact, like the very hybrid animals that we know from elsewhere in the ancient Near East.

Should you find yourself in the ancient Near Eastern wing of the British Museum or the Louvre or the Metropolitan Museum of Art or the Institute for the Study of Ancient Cultures at the University of Chicago, you'll quickly find yourself face to face with a massive creature carved into stone. Called a *lamassu*, these monumental figures, with the head of a human, the body of a bull, and wings, once stood in the royal palaces of ancient Assyria. They were often placed in pairs, flanking doorways, doing precisely the task of the biblical cherub: guarding and protecting the ruler within, keeping threats away. We have also found a number of ancient Phoenician thrones that depict winged lions on either side, supporting the throne (and the ruler who might sit on it).

The biblical cherub, that is to say, doesn't belong to the category of *angel*, be it biblical or the later Christian notion. It belongs, rather, to the ancient Near Eastern world and to the category of hybrid divine beings that served as royal guards. The difference is more than merely artistic.

Our understanding of God and of the divine beings that surround the deity has been shaped in essential and sometimes unnoticed ways by two millennia of Greco-Roman and Christian ideas. Both Judaism and Christianity developed hierarchies of angelic beings, with cherubs among them. Yet the divine realm of the Hebrew Bible emerged from, participated in, and looked a whole lot like those of the nations around them, from the early first millennium BCE.

The cherub—if we can get past the whole pudgy baby bit—is a reminder of just what God and the heavenly entourage looked like back then. If it is worlds away from what we imagine now, that should be no surprise. Our understandings of the divine were formed in a different cultural milieu. We like to think that we stand in continuity with the people and culture of the Bible, and in some ways we certainly do. But in many ways, and important ones, the world of the Bible is very foreign to us.

When we encounter a cherub in the text, then, we are faced with a choice: do we understand it as it once was, or as it might be to us now? To put it another way: do we go back to the biblical world, or do we bring the Bible into ours? Neither is right, and neither is wrong. It is, in a sense, in the negotiation between the two that we achieve a fuller understanding of both what the Bible is and where we stand in relation to it. The cherub, as it were, stands at the doorway between the biblical world and our own. And it's probably a little scary.

§ 7

Ark (ארון, *'aron*)

"You shall put into the ark the covenant that I shall give you."

Exodus 25:16 (NRSV)

IF THE MOVIES have taught us anything, it's that the ark of the covenant is a golden box with winged creatures on top and long poles for carrying and that if you open it a bunch of demonic ghost creatures will come out and kill you instantly. Some of this is entirely wrong (looking at you, demonic ghost creatures). Some of it is entirely right (box!). And some is only partially right. And that's because despite the preeminence of the ark as the most important ritual object in the holiest part of Israel's most sacred space, a thorough reader of the Bible might well be left in some confusion as to what it really is and what it really looked like. Unfortunately, this situation can't be cleared up—but it can be explained.

The first appearance in the Bible of the word ארון is the only time that it does not refer to that ark, the one we tend to call the "ark of the covenant." In Genesis 50:26, Joseph's embalmed body is placed into what virtually every translation renders, logically, "a coffin"—but the Hebrew word is ארון. While one occurrence shouldn't be taken to mean all that much, this might give us a sense of what an ארון was generically: that is, a box. The word itself doesn't demand any particular decoration, or form, or use. Which is to say: One can imagine all sorts of boxes. And the Bible does.

The ark we're used to envisioning, the one that's generally pretty well captured in *Raiders of the Lost Ark*, is the ark as described (thoroughly) in Exodus, in the priestly instructions for and construction of the Tabernacle and its furnishings. There, indeed, we find the box of acacia wood, plated with gold, the *cherubs* above, and the poles for carrying. This is the seat on which Yahweh sits, in his mobile sanctuary home. And inside of this priestly ark, according to the verse quoted above, is "the covenant." But, sadly, that translation is misleading. The word that is used here is not ברית, *b'rit*, which is the normal word for "*covenant*," but rather עדת, *'edut*, a word that seems to come from a root meaning "testify, witness" and the meaning of which, in this context, is generally agreed to be unknown. It is something tangible that Yahweh gives to Moses on top of Mount Sinai, but there is no description of it nor any sense of what it is supposed to signify even. The priestly text of the Pentateuch often calls it "the ark of the עדת" (see Exod 40:20, e.g.), but never "the ark of the ברית." At the heart of the priestly ark, then, is a mystery—but the rest of it is laid out in great detail.

The end of Numbers 10, not from the priestly source, gives us a somewhat different ark. Here the ark goes in front of the people, "to seek out a resting place for them" (Num 10:33), and there is a song about it, in which the ark seems to have a military function: "Arise, O Yahweh, let your enemies be scattered, and your foes flee before you" (10:35, NRSV). Here the ark seems to be imagined as a palanquin, carrying the deity before the Israelites into battle. This aspect of the ark is confirmed by another reference from the same pentateuchal source: after the episode of the spies in Numbers 14, the Israelites attempt to avoid the punishment of the wilderness by invading Canaan. They are doomed to fail, however, as Moses knows: "Do not go up, for the Lord is not with you" (Num 14:42, NRSV), he tells them. Yet they go anyway, "even though the ark of the covenant of the Lord had not left the camp" (14:44, NRSV). That is, the ark and Yahweh are coterminous, at least for military purposes. In this rendering of the ark, we know generally what it's for—but there is no physical description at all.

Turn to Deuteronomy, and we have yet a third ark. This one is a plain box of acacia wood—no gilding, no *cherubs*, no poles—and its function is to house the tablets of the Ten Commandments (Deut 10:2–5). At the end of the book, we're also told that the book of the *law*—that is, the laws of Deuteronomy itself—is to be placed beside the ark as a witness. The ark in Deuteronomy, therefore, is not where Yahweh is physically located, but is instead where the divinely ordained law—both the Ten Commandments and the laws given by Moses in Moab—are found. It is in Deuteronomy that we find the phrase "the ark of the covenant" with the word ברית, for it is here that the ark is the receptacle for the texts of the two *covenants* that Yahweh made with Israel in the wilderness.

Even within the first five books of the Bible, then, we have three distinct imaginings of the ark. That they don't agree suggests that the ark, as a sacred object, may in fact have existed more in the mind than in reality—or possibly, that as perhaps the most sacred of all Israelite ritual objects, it was largely inaccessible even to the biblical authors, forcing them to use their imaginations as they cast it back into the mythic past.

The ark gets its star turn in the biblical narrative in 1 Samuel 3–7, where, we read, it was captured by the Philistines and eventually returned to Israel (after it seemingly destroyed the Philistine idols and caused a plague among the Philistine people). In these chapters, the ark seems again to have a military function: When the Philistines learn that the ark is in the Israelite camp, they say "God has come into the camp" (1 Sam 4:7, JPS). It's also noteworthy that in this narrative it is always called "the ark of God" or "the ark of Yahweh," and never "the ark of the covenant." Later, in 2 Samuel, the ark will be moved again, by David, to Jerusalem, but not before a poor fellow named Uzzah accidentally touches it and is instantly killed. All this material in Samuel is sometimes referred to by scholars as "the ark narrative"—and whatever it is, it seems to present yet a fourth notion of the ark.

The ark is central, physically and conceptually, in the Bible. It is also ill-defined—fuzzy around the edges. And for all its prominence in the texts we've discussed and in our sense of Israel's sacred spaces and objects, it also is entirely absent from major swaths of the Bible. Yes, it is very much present from Exodus through Kings—that is, in the historical works. And it is certainly present in Chronicles. But outside of those books, it appears exactly twice: once in Jeremiah and once in Psalms. If we didn't have the historical books, we might never know that the ark ever existed. And even with the historical books, it's not entirely clear that it did.

At the end of the movie, of course, the ark is placed in another wooden box, and hidden away forever. The Bible is almost like a literary container for the ark. Even the biblical authors are seemingly forced to imagine what this thing was, and what it was for. We, two thousand-plus years later, need to remember that the ark of the Bible is not one thing; it is whatever each text makes it out to be. The physical center of Israelite religion is something of a shapeshifter, and we should be ready to change right along with it.

§ 8

Remember (זכר, *zakar*)

God heard their groaning, and God remembered his covenant with Abraham, Isaac, and Jacob.

Exodus 2:24 (NRSV)

Remembering is, at least in its conventional English usage, necessarily a secondary action. You can't remember unless you've first forgotten. If you haven't forgotten something, then you don't remember it—you just think about it. Strange, then, to find regularly in the Bible that God remembers. Noah in the midst of the flood (Gen 8:1), Abraham while Sodom and Gomorrah are being destroyed (Gen 19:29), the Israelites enslaved in Egypt (Exod 2:24), and more. We tend not to think of God as particularly forgetful; so it is surprising to hear of God remembering.

We need not hold to a belief that God is so perfect as to never forget anything in order to find these moments of remembering somewhat odd. Our perfected God isn't really to be found in the Bible. Even within the contours of the biblical story, it's pretty weird for God to have forgotten Noah while the flood is happening: for better or worse, there's literally nothing else going on, and no one else alive. Are we to think that God was so busy with everything else in the world that he forgot about Israel, his covenantal people, while they were suffering in Egypt?

Actually, there might be something wonderfully humbling about thinking so: we imagine ourselves to be the center of God's attention, but if even Israel in Egypt was forgotten, so too might we be. On the other hand, there's no question that Israel is the main character in its own biblical storytelling, and it's rather unlikely that the Bible's Israelite authors thought that their own national deity was off worrying about something other than them.

All that to say: "remember," with its implication of prior forgetting, is perhaps a misleading translation of the Hebrew זכר, at least much of the time. Take, for example, Jeremiah 14:10 (JPS): "Thus says Yahweh concerning his people: Truly they love to stray, they have not restrained their feet; so Yahweh has no pleasure in them. Now he will remember (זכר) their iniquity and punish their sin." In this verse, Yahweh is the one who declares that Israel has done wrong, and that he is unhappy with them. Yet "now" Yahweh will also remember their wrongdoing. There is no space for forgetting here, and thus זכר can hardly mean "remember" in its usual sense.

We are all aware that there is a difference between forgetting about something and simply not thinking about it in the moment. For the most part, we are capable of thinking about—really thinking about, concentrating on—only one thing at a time. Multitasking is hard! It isn't the case that whatever we aren't thinking about right this second has been forgotten. It has just been set aside momentarily. When we come back to it, it isn't really remembering. It is, instead, focusing: bringing it to the center of our attention. And that is what זכר really means.

The Psalms, where זכר appears a full fifty times, attest to this. "I זכר the days of old, I think about all your deeds, I meditate on the works of your hands" (Ps 143:5, NRSV). The parallel terms, "think about, meditate on" point not to "remember," but "concentrate, focus on." So too Psalm 8:4 (NRSV): "What are human beings that you should זכר them, mortals that you care for them?" The pleas found in the psalms for God to זכר the speaker may be best read not as "remember me, whom you have forgotten," but rather "I know you're busy, and therefore haven't been caring for me, but give me your attention now." And so too the converse: "Do not זכר the sins of my youth," as Psalm 25:7 (NRSV) says. Yes, there is recollection here, but more in the sense of "don't dwell on the past."

It isn't only God who "remembers," of course. Individuals "remember," but so too does Israel as a whole—or at least it's supposed to. "Remember that you were a slave in the land of Egypt," we read in Deuteronomy 15:15 (and a number of other times in Deuteronomy). In Deuteronomy, what is commanded to be "remembered" is indeed always something from Israel's past, which suggests the possibility of forgetting. "זכר the long way that the Lord your God has led you these forty years" (Deut 8:2, NRSV), for example. Israel might, at some point in the distant future, have legitimately forgotten how Yahweh sustained them in the wilderness. At the same time, what is at stake here is not just the retention of a memory, but the lesson learned from the past experience: "that man does not live on bread alone" (8:3, JPS). There is a thin line between memory and focus here. Israel need not have actually forgotten what Yahweh did for them to disregard it. And, given that Deuteronomy's primary argument is that Israel is inherently disobedient, the latter might be somewhat more apt.

What the זכר of God and of Israel have in common is that it is not mere thought, but also entails a corollary action. Whatever it is that is brought into focus is concentrated on not simply for the pleasure of contemplation but in order that something should happen. The psalmist pleads to be "remembered" so that Yahweh will rescue him. Israel is to "remember" so that they will correctly follow the *law*. God "remembers" Noah in the flood so that the waters subside; "remembers" Abraham so that Lot might be rescued; "remembers" Israel so that they might be taken out of Egypt. To "remember" is to focus on the past so as to make a difference in the present. "Remember" is an active verb.

§ 9

Passover (פסח, *pesach*)

"It is the passover sacrifice to the Lord, for he passed over the houses of the Israelites in Egypt, when he struck down the Egyptians but spared our houses."

Exodus 12:27 (NRSV)

IT'S ONE OF the great biblical puns, at least in English: the celebration of Passover because Yahweh "passed over"—get it?—the houses of the Israelites during the final plague in Egypt, the death of the firstborn. Of course, it's sort of a fake pun, since the word "Passover" isn't an actual English word. It was introduced to the language with William Tyndale's early sixteenth-century translation of the Bible into English, in which he needed a name for the festival and *sacrifice* that commemorated the Exodus and the moment when Yahweh "passed over" the Israelites to smite the Egyptians. Then again, if we go back to the Hebrew, the pun is very real indeed, as the same word, פסח, is used both as a noun for the *sacrifice* and as a verb for what Yahweh did. The only problem is that the verb probably didn't mean "pass over"—and so the *sacrifice* and festival, "Passover," are probably misnamed as well.

The noun, "Passover," occurs nearly fifty times in the Hebrew Bible and always refers to the *sacrifice* or festival introduced in Exodus 12. Outside of that chapter, there is never an explanation for why it has this name. Even Deuteronomy 16—which is the chronologically, if not canonically, earliest reference to פסח—doesn't say that it should be celebrated because Yahweh "passed over" the houses of the Israelites. It simply connects the timing of the פסח to the month of Abib, when Israel left Egypt, and ties the eating of unleavened bread to the hasty departure. Actually, the absence of an explanation in Deuteronomy 16 may be an important clue for us.

What Deuteronomy 16 makes clear is that there are really two things going on at the same time: a *sacrifice* called פסח that isn't explained but is timed to the Exodus, and the practice of not eating leaven, which lasts for a week and is grounded in the Exodus story. These two rites may be simultaneous, but they aren't one rite and are certainly not one and the same. We can see this in Exodus 12, too: Verses 2–14 are entirely about the lamb that is to be used for the פסח *sacrifice*, while verses 15–20 are entirely about the unleavened bread, with no mention of the *sacrifice*; verses 21–28 are again entirely about the פסח. And to add a further piece to the puzzle, in the earliest of the Bible's festival calendars, in Exodus 23:14–17, there's no mention of the פסח at all. There's only "the festival of unleavened bread"—and here it's the unleavened bread, rather than the פסח sacrifice, that's explicitly tied to the month of Abib when Israel came out of Egypt.

What's happening here is a pretty standard process. Israel's festivals were originally all agricultural, tied to the harvest calendar. The arrival of the new grain, the early harvest, the late harvest—these were the occasions on which Israelites would go to their local sanctuaries and offer thanks to Yahweh. Gradually, these agricultural celebrations would become tied to moments in Israel's mythic history: the new grain (unleavened bread) to the Exodus, the early harvest (Shavuot) to the giving of the law at Sinai, the late harvest (Sukkot) to Yahweh's sustenance of Israel in the wilderness. All fine—but none of these is actually the פסח.

That's because there's something different about the פסח. All of these other festivals share not only their agricultural origins but also their seven-day celebrations. But the פסח is only a single day—in fact, it's nothing more than a single sacrificial offering. It's certainly possible that someone instituted a *sacrifice* for the purpose of celebrating the moment that Yahweh successfully avoided killing all of Israel's firstborn. But it's more likely that it's the other way around: that there was a sacrifice known as the פסח, and that it was, like the three major festivals we've already discussed, secondarily linked with the Exodus story. That, at least, would explain why Deuteronomy doesn't feel the need to explain the name of the *sacrifice*—it would have already existed and been well known to Deuteronomy's audience—but does need to explain how it is related to the Exodus.

So what is this פסח thing, then, if it isn't originally related to either the festival of unleavened bread or to the Exodus story? Here, admittedly, we run into a bit of a block. None of the verses that use the noun פסח are helpful, since they're all based on either Deuteronomy or Exodus. So we have to turn to the verb. Leaving aside the times it's used in Exodus 12, which just take us in a logical circle, there are only four other places it appears. One of them is related to a different noun (albeit one that is spelled the same), which means "lame," and refers to Mephibosheth, who was dropped as a child and crippled (יפסח). Two others occur in the conflict between Elijah and the prophets of Baal, where it seems to mean "hop" (and is almost certainly related to the "lame" root). None of those meanings works particularly well. But in Isaiah 3:5 (JPS), we find this: "Like the birds that fly, even so will the Lord of Hosts shield Jerusalem, shielding and saving, protecting and rescuing." Our פסח word is hidden in there: it's the word "protecting."

That's probably the original meaning of the word פסח: "to protect." It's likely that there was an annual *sacrifice* called פסח that was meant to either thank Yahweh for protecting Israel over the past year or to encourage Yahweh to protect Israel for the next (or both). Like the major festivals, this sacrifice was eventually understood to have a historical referent. When did Yahweh most prominently protect Israel? Deuteronomy, naturally, chose the Exodus, generally speaking. The author of Exodus 12 got more specific: not just the Exodus as a whole, but the precise moment when Yahweh could have killed the Israelites but didn't: at the death of the firstborn. That was when Yahweh protected—not passed over—Israel.

The pun still works. It's just that we should be calling the holiday "Protection" rather than "Passover," because Yahweh "protected the houses of the Israelites." It's a small thing, maybe. But getting back to the original sense of the word might remind us that in ancient Israel there was much to worry about, and much to be protected from, beyond that one long-ago incident. The Exodus story may be the paradigmatic example of Yahweh's protection, but it is the protection more generally, then and since, that is to be celebrated.

§ 10

Most High (עליון, *'elyon*)

King Melchizedek of Salem brought out bread and wine; he was priest of God Most High.

Genesis 14:18 (NRSV)

IT'S NOT THE etymology that's at issue here: עליון certainly comes from the root עלה, "to go up." Nor is it the translation: "Most High" is a perfectly reasonable, and quite ancient, rendering of the word. What makes עליון worthy of inclusion in this collection, rather, is its referent. Because while we hear "Most High" as an epithet of Yahweh, Israel's god, it was originally used to refer to another deity altogether—and that use is still visible even within the Bible.

That's not to say, of course, that "Most High" isn't often used as a title for Yahweh. "The Lord [Yahweh] thundered from heaven, the Most High uttered his voice," we read in 2 Samuel 22:14 (NRSV), where the parallelism makes clear that Yahweh and "the Most High" are one and the same. Or in Psalms: "I will sing praise to the name of the Lord [Yahweh], the Most High" (Ps 7:17, NRSV). The psalms are full of עליון, the vast majority of them clearly titles for Israel's god.

But then there are some that, well, aren't. The case of Melchizedek, quoted in the epigraph above, is a good example. It would be rather strange if Melchizedek were a priest of Israel's god Yahweh—according to the story, after all, there's no one else in the world who worships

Yahweh aside from Abraham and his family; and there aren't any priests of Yahweh in the story until later in the book of Exodus. Nor does Melchizedek ever say the name Yahweh. When he blesses Abraham, he says "Blessed be Abram by God Most High, maker of heaven and earth, and blessed be God Most High" (Gen 14:19–20, NRSV). Not Yahweh Most High, but God Most High, El Elyon. El may be the generic word for "god" in basically every Semitic language, but it's also the name of the chief deity of the Canaanite pantheon, the father of the storm god Baal, understood in Canaanite myth to be, indeed, the creator of the heavens and the earth, just as Yahweh is in Genesis 1. Melchizedek is a Canaanite priest—it's only natural that he should follow a Canaanite god. And we don't need to speculate as to whether the epithet "Elyon" is also Canaanite. A list of deities from an eighth-century BCE Aramaic treaty includes the name עלין, "Elyon." There is evidence that the Phoenicians, too, worshipped a deity called "Elioun."

Two other biblical passages seem to reflect Canaanite myths about this chief god, El Elyon. In Deuteronomy 32:8 (NRSV), we read about how "the Most High apportioned the nations, when he divided humankind." This refers to a Canaanite creation story in which humans were created and placed into their various territories, their nations. Each nation was then attached to a deity that would serve as its national patron god: "He fixed the boundaries of the peoples according to the number of the gods," the verse continues. (A later Hebrew scribe, uncomfortable with this foreign myth, changed "gods" at the end to "Israelites," which doesn't really make any sense at all; the original "gods" remains in the Greek translation, the Septuagint, as well as in the Dead Sea Scrolls.) And as if to prove that Yahweh isn't the one doing the distributing, the next verse tells us that "the Lord's [Yahweh's] portion was his people, Jacob his allotted share" (Deut 32:9, NRSV). Yahweh is receiving; Elyon, the high god of Canaanite religion, is doing the giving out.

Similarly, in Psalm 82 we read about Yahweh's conflict with other deities, whom he accuses of judging improperly and therefore being unworthy of the status of gods. Yahweh stands in the divine council, surrounded by other deities, and lays out his charges (Ps 82:2–5). Then he addresses the other deities directly: "You are gods, children of the Most High, all of you" (82:6, NRSV). Again we can see the Canaanite background, in which El Elyon was the high god, and the progenitor of all the lesser gods. Yahweh cannot be identical with "the Most High" here—unless we want to make this a psalm about Yahweh demoting his own offspring, which opens an even more challenging can of worms.

The epithet "Most High," therefore, originates, even in the Bible, in a time when polytheism was perfectly acceptable, when Canaanite deities and the myths about them still held some cultural currency. Of course, that time would pass. As Yahweh gradually transformed from the localized patron deity of Israel into the universal god of the entire world, he took on (or was given) features of other deities, such as the storm-god nature of Baal (see, e.g., Ps 29). And, in the case of "the Most High," he also took on the names or epithets of other deities, assimilating them. Yahweh taking on El's title of עליון is not just nomenclature; it is a statement of Yahweh's growing stature. Ironically, calling Yahweh "the Most High" both sets him above all other deities and serves as a reminder that he was once a deity like any other.

Intermezzo

§ 11

And (ו, *ve-*)

And God said, Let there be light.

Genesis 1:3 (KJV)

THOUGH WE MAY imitate the language of the King James Bible by using the typical Elizabethan words and suffixes—"thee," "thou," "saith," and so on—no element of the KJV has been more persistent in subsequent translations, indeed has become nearly synonymous with the very sound of the Bible in English, than the use of the word "And" at the beginning of nearly every sentence. In Genesis 1 alone, the KJV begins a sentence with "And" a full 32 times—more times than there are even verses in the chapter.

When we hear someone reading a text in which every sentence begins "And," we know almost automatically that it is the Bible. No other text, ancient or modern, seems to be this way. The extraordinarily repetitive use of "And" isn't without reason—but it's also not exactly right, either.

In Hebrew, the word "and" is a single letter, *vav*: ו. As the conjunction, it operates exactly as it does in English, though it can also have a wider range of meanings. Hebrew has fewer words than English, and many of its smaller words—particles, prepositions—serve to represent clusters of ideas. So *vav* can mean "and," but it can also mean "or," "but," and "while," among others, depending on the context.

The same letter, however, is also used at the beginning of the most common verbal form in Biblical Hebrew. In the example above, "And God said," the verb is *vayyomer*, and the first letter is *vav*. But—despite being the same letter used for the word "and"—it doesn't really mean "*and* God said." The *vav* is, in layman's terms, the part of the verb that marks it as being the next thing that happens in the narrative sequence. Without the *vav*, what remains, *yomer*, would mean "he will say." The attentive reader will also note the doubled *y*: not *veyomer*, which is what we would expect from the simple conjunction "and," but *vayyomer*. This is no normal "and."

Though no exact analogy is available in English, we might imagine a world in which there were an English word *ed*. Now if someone were to translate every past tense verb in English thinking that the suffix *-ed* both marks the past tense and requires its own translation, we'd end up with something rather ridiculous. Just such silliness is what is happening in translations of Hebrew that both render *wayyomer* in the past tense (i.e., "he said") and also put the word "and" in front of it. The *vav* isn't doing double duty: the word *wayyomer* means "he said," and nothing more.

To put it another way: in Biblical Hebrew, you can't narrate a sequence of past events without using the verbal form that begins with a *vav*. But in English, of course, you can—and, in fact, we all do, all the time. When we tell stories, we don't begin every sentence with "and." We allow the internal logic of the events to communicate the sequence. "God said, Let there be light, and there was light. God saw that the light was good; then God separated the light from the darkness. God called the light Day, while the darkness he called Night. There was evening and there was morning, the first day." We don't need "and" at the beginning of every clause to understand what is happening. Sometimes it is appropriate—but when is determined by the context. Sometimes we might add the word "then" to ensure that the movement of the story is clear. Sometimes we might use a semi-colon. All of these are our modern conventions for narrative—and none of them are actually present in the Hebrew.

At stake here is both a question about how Biblical Hebrew works and a decision about how we translate the Bible into modern English. To render the *vav* at the beginning of these verbs as "and" is to misunderstand Biblical Hebrew. It is a kind of hyper-accurate representation, mistaking part of a verbal form for an independent word. It also, however, results in a specifically "biblical" sort of syntax, one that is unique to this text among all literature. Though there is certainly a case to be made for recognizing the specialness of the Bible as a literary work, we should also remember that for the ancient Israelite authors, the language they wrote in wasn't "biblical." It was just Hebrew, the same that they spoke, the same that they used when writing letters to each other that they never imagined would be preserved for posterity. When we translate the Bible into English, we shouldn't make its language more exceptional to our ears than it would have been to theirs. Biblical Hebrew was to them what English is to us: native and natural. The stilted use of "and" in translations of the Bible is wrong—wrong on the grammar, and wrong on the language.

II

Words Connected to People

§ 12

Soul (נפש, *nefesh*)

To you, O Lord, I lift up my soul.

Psalm 25:1 (NRSV)

THE SOUL, BY most reckonings, is that which makes a person a person, an individual, a life. This is certainly true in most of Western thought for the past two millennia (and more): without the soul, the body is but a lump of clay, unmoved and unmotivated. This body-soul divide has been an aspect of how people think about themselves from Plato down to Descartes, which is to say, from antiquity to modernity. The term נפש in the Hebrew Bible is traditionally translated "soul," and it does, often at least, share the basic concept: the נפש is the essence of a person. Where the נפש differs from the usual sense of "soul" is that it is not so easily separable from the body.

The base meaning of the Hebrew נפש is, in fact, a part of the body: the throat. In a few passages it is used in exactly this anatomical sense. Don't eat the food of those who are stingy, Proverbs tells us, "for like a hair in the throat (נפש), so are they" (Prov 23:7, NRSV). It's a wonderfully evocative image, a feeling that all are familiar with—and a phrase that doesn't work at all if we took it as "like a hair in the soul." Jeremiah admonishes his audience to "Keep your feet from going unshod and your throat (נפש) from thirst" (Jer 2:25, NRSV). The message may be metaphorical, but the metaphor only works if the נפש is as physical as the feet.

Once we begin to recognize the metaphorical use of נפש, as playing in the space between the physical throat and metaphorical "thirst," we may begin to read in a more nuanced way some passages that have come to us in English as being about the "soul." "My נפש thirsts for God," says Psalm 42:2. If read in translation as "my soul thirsts for God," as is common, we may correctly understand the intent: my very being desires closeness with the deity. But we may also miss the tangible side: my throat thirsts for God, as if parched. "You have delivered my נפש from death, and my feet from falling" (Ps 56:13, NRSV). If it is "my soul" that is delivered, the pairing with "feet" is somewhat awkward. With the soul delivered, what do the feet matter? But if it is the throat that is delivered from death, then the parallelism works merismatically: it is the whole person, from top to bottom, from throat to feet, that is saved. "My נפש is satisfied as with a rich feast, and my mouth praises you with joyful lips" (Ps 63:5, NRSV). "Like cold water to a thirsty נפש" (Prov 25:25, NRSV). To read these, and many other biblical verses, with a dualistic idea of "soul" versus body is to miss what makes these texts tick.

The נפש is often associated with desire. "You shall reign over all that your נפש desires" (1 Kgs 11:37, NRSV). "My נפש longs for you, O God" (Ps 42:1, NRSV). "My נפש is consumed with longing" (Ps 119:20, NRSV). Desire is motivation—it is the force that moves the body, whether it is a desire for the most basic of human needs or for an abstract divine sustenance. Schopenhauer would call it the will, the innermost essence of every being, and the aspect that survives even after the body in which it is housed has ceased to be: that is, the soul. Yet by rooting this idea in the throat, in the נפש, the Hebrew recognizes that desire begins in the body. It is felt physically, it moves from the inside outward.

This is true not just of desire, but of all emotions. A rather remarkable verse in the psalms reads: "Be gracious to me, O Yahweh, for I am in distress; my eye wastes away from grief, my soul and body also" (Ps 31:9, NRSV). Eye, soul, and body is something of a strange trio—but when we realize that the Hebrew here literally says "my throat (נפש) and my belly (בטן) also," it makes more sense. Now the psalmist is describing the way that grief and distress manifest in the body: in the weeping of the eye, the tightening of the throat, the pit in the belly.

Just as in English, נפש can be used simply to designate a person. We might talk about the number of souls lost in a shipwreck, for example. So too the Bible: "The total number of persons (נפש) that were of Jacob's issue came to seventy" (Exod 1:5, JPS). Again, we shouldn't lose sight of the bodily origins of the word. This isn't a case of the intangible soul being used to refer to the body in which it is housed. It's the other way around: it's a part of the body being used synechdochically to refer to the whole; it's the equivalent of the English phrase "head count," with "throat" in place of "head."

The נפש may be lifted up to God, as in the epigraph above—though here, as so often, we might consider that this is more physical than is usually thought: the equivalent of lifting one's voice, one's throat, to God. It is also often understood to be what goes down to Sheol, the underworld, after death. "You have delivered my נפש from the depths of Sheol" (Ps 86:13, NRSV). "If Yahweh had not been my help, my נפש would soon have lived in the land of silence" (Ps 94:17, NRSV). Here we, with our modern sensibilities, are particularly susceptible to misunderstanding. For we tend to imagine the underworld, or the afterlife, as a realm of the *spirit*, not of the body, which, after all, is decaying right here on earth. Yet ancient Israelites were less clear on that. Those in Sheol seem to be there quite physically, with their hair, their armor, their clothing.

From the throat to desire to a person in their entirety, נפש can take on a wide range of meanings. And it certainly can, at times, lean toward the ideas associated with the modern notion of a "soul." But it is rarely if ever totally disembodied. This biblical word serves to remind us that the body-soul dualism that has dominated Western thought for two millennia isn't natural or obvious—and that it may prevent us from seeing, and feeling, all that the Bible has to offer.

§ 13

Spirit (רוח, *ruach*)

And the Spirit of God moved upon the face of the waters.

Genesis 1:2 (KJV)

In its translation of Genesis 1:2, the KJV implicitly puts forward a pretty substantial theological claim, with its capitalized "Spirit of God." Many devout trinitarians will find here a not-so-subtle reference to the Holy Spirit, and that may well be what the KJV translators had in mind. One need not be firmly trinitarian, however, to see here some notion of a divine aspect, or perhaps a divine being, somehow separate and separable from God. The text could just have said "God moved upon the face of the waters"—"Spirit" here must be meaningful in some way.

Like "*soul,*" "spirit" has often been understood in distinction to "body." A person is composed of a physical form that grows and perishes, but within it is the "spirit," the person's essence, their true being. The flesh may fail, but the spirit remains. But—like "*soul*"—the Hebrew word and concept standing behind the English translation "spirit," רוח, is more physical than metaphysical.

The Hebrew word רוח means "breath"—as, of course, does the Latin root from which the English "spirit" is derived: *spiritus,* as in "respiration," among other words. The word רוח is, perhaps, onomatopoetic: *ruach*. It can refer to the breath of humans: "They have ears, but they hear not; neither is there any breath (רוח) in their mouths" (Ps 135:17, KJV). It can also be the breath of God: "The foundations of the earth were laid bare at the rebuke of the Lord, at the blast of the breath (רוח) of his nostrils" (2 Sam 22:16, NRSV). In cases like this, where "spirit" doesn't really work, even the KJV renders the word as "breath." We might, however, consider other passages where "spirit" is possible, but "breath" does some important work. The KJV gives Genesis 6:3 as "My spirit shall not always strive with man, for that he also is flesh." The NRSV amends slightly: "My spirit shall not abide in mortals forever, for they are flesh." And the JPS goes literal: "My breath shall not abide in man forever, since he too is flesh." It is only in this last translation that we hear, I think correctly, echoes of the idea that human life is made possible by the divine breath that is breathed into each individual. Life begins with the intake of breath and ends with its exhalation—any ancient Israelite audience would immediately hear that in this verse, but a modern reader encountering the word "spirit" might well not.

The same is true of Genesis 1:2: the "breath" of God can be understood as "wind" (as many modern translations have it). Or, more obviously, in Isaiah 40:7, "The grass withereth, the flower fadeth; because the spirit (רוח) of the Lord bloweth upon it," reads the KJV. Here, surely, "breath" or "wind" is what blows upon grass and flowers. When Moses speaks to the Israelites in Exodus 6:9, they do not listen to him: In the KJV, it is "for anguish of spirit (רוח)," which captures perhaps the Israelites' internal feeling; other translations similarly have "because of their broken spirit" (NRSV) or "their spirits crushed" (JPS). The literal meaning here, however, is "from shortness of breath (רוח)"—the Israelites have been worked so hard that they can hardly breathe, much less believe that their enslavement is almost at an end.

Breath is literally enlivening; it is a small step to the metaphorical. One's רוח, "spirit," is what gives a person impetus to act. Yet there are different types of spirits: a "spirit of jealousy" (Num 5:14); a "spirit of wisdom" (Deut 34:9); a "spirit of judgment" (Isa 28:6). The spirit can be sad or angry; energized or weakened. Without pushing too hard on the bodily over the metaphorical, we might consider the ways that our breath reflects our mental state. Often we hear of a troubled spirit or of a spirit that is overwhelmed or failing—while these certainly describe emotional states, they also call on the physical, embodied experience of breathing. Ragged breath, shallow breath, shortness of breath—these are the physical manifestations of emotion (or, perhaps, vice versa). "Hear me speedily, O Lord: my spirit (רוח) faileth" (Ps 143:7, KJV). "I can hardly breathe" is the embodied sensation expressed here by the Hebrew but harder to detect in the English.

Breath, and spirit, is internal to the human; it comes from within. But it also goes out, and in the Bible there is both the inner spirit and the spirit that is imposed from without. The latter is, almost without exception, the divine spirit. The only human spirit that is ever shared with another human is that of Elijah, passed on to his disciple Elisha—and even that is a pretty divine spirit. Otherwise it is the spirit of God/Yahweh that comes over humans. The spirit of God can be on people, and it can be in them; there seems little difference. Prophets bear the spirit of God; the spirit of Yahweh comes over the judges; the craftsman Bezalel has it, as will the messiah envisioned in Isaiah 11:2. The divine spirit rests on and in people, but not inertly: Just as breath oxidizes the blood and permits the exercise of muscles, so, too, the divine spirit gives the recipient the power to act: to lead, to fight, to prophesy. "The spirit of the Lord rushed on him, and he went down to Ashkelon and killed thirty men of the town" (Judg 14:19, NRSV). "The spirit of the Lord will possess you, and you will be in a prophetic frenzy" (1 Sam 10:6, NRSV). The spirit of God is an activating one.

All this to say: the spirit, רוח, in the Bible is not separable from one's body. It comes from within—and even when it comes from without, it came from God's within. It is what moves us, literally and figuratively. Breath, spirit—רוח is the motivating force in our lives, that which drives us to act, that urges us forward, like wind in a sail.

§ 14

Slave/Servant (עבד, *'eved*)

We were slaves to Pharaoh in Egypt.

Deuteronomy 6:21 (JPS)

THE ENGLISH WORDS "servant" and "slave" have decidedly different connotations. "Servant" has the sense of "employee." "Slave," by contrast, carries with it the ideas of an owned and controlled body, of violence and dishonor. The connotation of "servant" can verge on the positive; "slave" is predominantly negative. How a reader of the Bible understands the identity of a character or the relationship between one character and another or the world of ancient Israel depends significantly on whether the word "servant" or "slave" is used. In Hebrew, however, there is but one word underlying every occurrence of "servant" and "slave" in our modern translations. The distinction between the two exists only on the level of interpretation.

It is not a matter of mere nomenclature. Take the story of Genesis 24, in which Abraham sends his servant off to find a wife for Isaac. The servant—though the main character of the passage—has no name and is identified only by his title, which he even uses to introduce himself: "I am Abraham's servant," he says (Gen 24:34, JPS). This is often read as a warm story about a devoted servant—usually imagined to be relatively old—who carries out the elderly patriarch's final wishes. How does it change, how do we reimagine it, when we read all thirteen mentions of Abraham's servant as, in fact, Abraham's slave? We know Abraham has slaves: His "servant" even says so in this very chapter in the very next verse: "The Lord has greatly blessed my master, and he has become rich: he has given him sheep and cattle, silver and gold, male and female slaves, camels and asses" (24:35, JPS). Yet generations of translators, interpreters, and readers have failed to connect the slaves (the property with which God has blessed Abraham) and the servant—the slave who is the protagonist of this same story.

When slaves are turned into servants, the Bible itself is changed. Our revulsion at the institution of slavery is kept at a distance from the biblical text that stands as our religious heritage. The Bible is protected, albeit from itself. Slavery is minimized, or worse: The King James Version, notably, does not translate עבד as "slave" a single time. The result? Some KJV readers have denied that there is any slavery in the Bible whatsoever. Yet the word עבד appears around 800 times in the Bible. That's 800 moments when a slave, and the existence of slavery in ancient Israel and the biblical text, has been erased.

The social role that we associate with the term "servant" didn't exist in ancient Israel. Slaves, however, did. Israel knew what it was to be a slave, and Israel knew, too, what it was to own a slave. And thus Israel uses the language and metaphor of slavery again and again to express the basic notions of obedience, of power disparity, of bodily control and the absence of agency. Samuel says to Yahweh upon being called, "Speak, Lord, for your servant is listening" (1 Sam 3:9, JPS). "Let my lord go ahead of his servant," Jacob says to Esau in Genesis 33:14 (JPS). Rendered as "servant" in every translation, this is a sort of formally obsequious, self-abnegating speech. While literal slavery is not at stake in these sorts of expressions, the metaphorical reference to the relative status of slave and master is lost when it is translated as "servant."

So, too, when those figures who are the עבד to a king are referred to as "courtiers," "officials," "attendants," "soldiers," "subjects," "envoys," "ministers," or even sometimes simply "men," of the king. These are all translations of the same word, and the instinct to specify their distinctive roles in the royal court is understandable. Yet in doing so, translations obscure the actual language with the connotations that it presents: subordination, threat of violence to one's person, absolute control over will and agency. And so, too, when it is not a human king but God to whom one is said to be עבד. In the book of Joshua, God states, "My servant Moses is dead" (1:2, JPS)—we are relatively comfortable with the idea of serving God but perhaps less so with the idea of being God's slave. Yet the qualities of obedience, subservience, and loyalty—and the implicit threat of punishment for the lack thereof—are part of this picture as well. One might point to the way this language is picked up in the New Testament in the phrase "slave of Christ" in 1 Corinthians 7:22.

If "servants" and "slaves" are not understood to be equivalent—and in modern English it is safe to say that they are not—then every time that the word עבד appears, a choice has to be made by the translator. The diminishment of the very word "slave" in English translations of the Hebrew Bible results in the diminishment of the idea and reality of slavery in the Bible and in the world that produced it. Though there is no debate to be had about whether there was slavery in the Bible and in ancient Israel, a lay reader of the text in translation might well wonder.

Our ears, and eyes, have become accustomed to seeing the word "servant" in the Bible. "Slave" often sounds wrong, inapt, almost harsh. Yet it is just this discomfort that signals how important the change is. Whenever we encounter the word "servant" in our English translations, we should be obliged to ask why it says "servant" and not "slave"—and what difference it would make to our reading of the text as an individual, as a community, and as a culture if we were instead to read "slave."

§ 15

Vanity (הבל, *hevel*)

Vanity of vanities, saith the Preacher, vanity of vanities; all is vanity.
Ecclesiastes 1:2 (KJV)

THE OPENING LINES of Ecclesiastes, as rendered by the King James Version, are perhaps the most famous use of the word "vanity" in the English language. As any reader knows, this is the central keyword for the entire book of Ecclesiastes, appearing twenty-eight times in its twelve chapters, and in every chapter but one. But modern English no longer uses the word "vanity" the way that the translators of the KJV intended it. The biblical text that suggests that we all "eat, drink, and be merry" is hardly the one to level charges of self-centeredness.

The Hebrew term translated as "vanity" here is הבל. The word probably had an original meaning of "breath" but is used everywhere to suggest two broad concepts: ephemerality—as in the fleeting quality of a breath—and worthlessness. The first of these overlaps with our modern notion of "vanishing"; the second with the phrase "in vain." Both terms, "vanish" and "vain"—and also, of course, "vanity"—come from the same Latin root, *vanus*, meaning "empty." And that is how the KJV translation intended this to read: all is fleeting, worthless, in vain.

Many commentators (sometimes to their chagrin) take Ecclesiastes to be saying that everything in life is meaningless. While there may be some nihilism lurking in the darker corners of the book, the "meaning" of life is not really what is at issue here. It's probably safe to say that the entire notion of "the meaning of life" is pretty foreign to the Hebrew Bible as a whole. What we call the wisdom books—Proverbs, Ecclesiastes, and Job—are concerned less with what life means and more with how to live it properly, and, perhaps above all, with how we can know how to live it properly.

Ecclesiastes uses "vanity" in both of its main senses: "Who knows what is good for mortals while they live the few days of their vain (הבל) life, which they pass like a shadow?" (Eccl 6:12, NRSV). The allusion to the passing of a shadow suggests that here the sense is not vain as in futile—at least not primarily—but as in fleeting. Frequently Ecclesiastes refers to the speaker's, or someone else's, "vain life." This is the same idea we find in, for example, Psalms 144:4 (NRSV); what are humans? "They are like a breath (הבל), their days like a passing shadow."

Though disguised as a proper name, perhaps the best manifestation of this ephemeral term is in the story of Cain and the brother he kills, the brother who never speaks a word, who exists in the story only to pass swiftly from it: Abel, or, as he's known in Hebrew, הבל.

Life is fleeting—this is an important part of the message of Ecclesiastes. But just as importantly, perhaps, the attempt to figure out how life works—how one should live properly, why some people suffer and some succeed, and especially how we may behave in this life so as to ensure a blessed existence in the next—is worthless, futile, in vain.

This is not to say that such efforts are meaningless. It is, rather, that they result in no benefit. It is in this sense of the word that הבל comes to be used, especially in the prophetic books, to refer to idols and foreign gods. Whether other gods exist or not—and this is a question that different parts of the Bible have different answers to—it is the consistent claim of the Hebrew Bible that they will not provide for Israel the way that Israel's god does.

Turning to foreign gods means hoping for some sort of advantage from them; it means not trusting in the providence of God. "What wrong did your fathers find in me that they abandoned me," Jeremiah asks (Jer 2:5, JPS). "They turned to הבלs"—looking for something that might give them what they felt they lacked from God. But this is seeking in vain. Jeremiah goes on to give us the perfect definition of a הבל: "there is no profit in them" (Jer 16:19).

What Ecclesiastes gives us, then, is a pessimistic perspective not on life itself but rather on the effort to understand it. Or, more to the point: Ecclesiastes, by declaring that effort to be הבל, proclaims that the desire to gain an advantage—to decode the behaviors or attitudes by which one might ensure a more blessed existence in this world or the next—is akin to idolatry. It is God, whose ways are unknowable, who decides our fates. Any system we can construct, any philosophical edifice we can erect, is an attempt to superimpose our own human logic on the divine will. Such attempts are הבל: there is no profit in them.

§ 16

Unclean/Impure (טמא, *tame'*)

You are to distinguish between the holy and the common, and between the unclean and the clean.

Leviticus 10:10 (NRSV)

UNCLEAN, IMPURE—THEY SOUND like dirty words. In some cultures, they are: The dalit caste in India is considered unclean and untouchable and unfit for any but the least desirable social roles. The biblical association of uncleanness and *leprosy*, in particular, has contributed to the notion that impurity is linked to a sense of disgust or physical avoidance. Impurity, it would seem, is a state that no one would ever want to find themselves in.

Chances are, though, that you are unclean, at least in biblical terms, right this moment. Impurity, it turns out, is rather difficult to avoid on a day-to-day basis. This is especially so if you're a woman, as menstruation causes impurity. But banal, everyday tasks, like removing that dead mouse from under the stove, also make you unclean. What's more, essential parts of human existence, both biological and social, cause impurity too: giving birth and burying the dead, the two ends of the life cycle.

Certainly in ancient Israel, most people would have been impure almost all the time. And despite our contemporary sense of stigma around uncleanness or impurity, this was perfectly fine. They understood that being unclean was normal. It's purity that's the unusual human condition. And purity is required only in one single circumstance: if you want to interact with someone, something, or somewhere *sacred*. What we refer to simply as impurity or uncleanness is, in fact, limited to a very restricted sphere of life. It is, more properly, cultic impurity—ritual uncleanness.

While common, non-sacred objects and people can be pure or impure, it is unacceptable for the sacred and the impure to come into contact. If you devote yourself to be a nazirite, like Samson, taking the burden of holiness onto yourself, you must avoid impurity (Judg 13:4). Those who carry the sacred vessels of the Temple must also remain clean (Isa 52:11). When Isaiah sees God, he is terrified not only by his proximity to the deity but by the fact that he has brought impurity, uncleanness, into the divine sphere: "I am lost, for I am a man of unclean lips!" (Isa 6:5, NRSV). Before God appears on Mount Sinai, the Israelites are instructed to purify themselves, as they will be in the presence of the deity (Exod 19:10).

Ritual impurity, at least as conceived in Leviticus and similar priestly biblical texts, is not an abstract concept, but a real, tangible—if invisible—entity in the world. Whatever its origins, it is attracted to and contaminates the sacred sphere, God's sanctuary. Many of the rituals in Leviticus are designed to eliminate impurities from the sanctuary: the sanctuary is God's home, his dwelling place in the midst of the Israelites, and it is imperative to ensure his continued presence and protection by keeping his home as clean as possible.

Thus before coming to offer a *sacrifice* one must be pure. Before eating a sacrificial meal, one must be pure—this is why Saul assumes that David must be impure when David fails to attend the feast of the new moon (1 Sam 20:26). Obviously the priests, who are constantly in the *sacred* space, touching *sacred* objects, eating *sacred* food, and who themselves are consecrated, must do everything in their power to avoid impurity. They alone are forbidden to bury a dead relative or to come near a corpse, even of their own parent (Lev 21:1, 11).

For the average Israelite, however, none of this would have been of any regular concern. They went to the sanctuary quite rarely: "Three times a year all your males shall appear before the Lord God" (Exod 23:17, NRSV). Impurity—essentially the natural state of humanity—wouldn't have interfered with their daily lives at all. At the same time, impurity left unremedied could potentially contaminate the sanctuary even from a distance. So it couldn't just be ignored.

Fortunately, most of the common forms of ritual uncleanness are eliminated simply by bathing. This, too, reinforces the notion that impurity wasn't a particularly big deal: Eliminating it required only some basic hygienic practices. There is a historical irony here, however. Because of the purity laws, Jews in the Middle Ages bathed more frequently than their Christian neighbors. As a result, when the Black Death struck Europe in the fourteenth century, Jews had a higher survival rate. This unfortunately led Christians to believe that the plague had been caused by Jews and thus to massacre many Jewish communities.

The incompatibility of impurity and the sacred can lead to a sense that uncleanness is an affront to God, that God despises the impure person. Even in the Bible impurity comes to be used as a metaphor to describe distance from God or God's will: Idolatry, for example, is equated with impurity by Ezekiel (Ezek 20:18, e.g.). But we should be careful not to confuse the metaphor with the reality. People could and did become impure on a nearly daily basis; at certain important life moments, it was necessary, even important, that one would become impure.

The stigma against impurity is not a biblical one. Impurity was not an existential state; it was a passing one, often remedied by mere bathing, and it was relevant only insofar as it restricted a person's ability to go to the sanctuary. Unless you were a priest, it was perfectly acceptable to become impure. It was expected, it was natural, and it was entirely removed from any moral judgment.

§ 17

Fear (ירא, *yare'*)

The fear of the Lord is the beginning of wisdom.

Proverbs 9:10 (NRSV)

Early in my studies, it was explained to me that when we find the phrase "the fear of the Lord," or "the fear of God" in the Bible it isn't meant to be taken literally. What is expressed in these words, I was told, isn't fear, exactly, but rather respect, reverence, awe. Modern translations, working with the same understanding, will occasionally render the word ירא as one of those alternatives: "Revere the Lord your God" (Deut 10:12, JPS), or "God has done this so that all should stand in awe before him" (Eccl 3:14, NRSV), or "You shall not pay reverence to the gods of the Amorites" (Judg 6:10, NRSV). Surely these notions are part of the biblical meaning of "fear." But are they primary? In something of a reversal of the usual procedure, here I want to suggest that the meaning we have lost over time is actually the one that still appears (most of the time) on the surface of our Bibles today. What has been obscured is the actual fear that stands behind the fear of the Lord.

One can understand the desire to take "fear" less than literally when it comes to God. This is, after all, the word that is used when Israel sees the Egyptians bearing down on them in the wilderness (Exod 14:10) and when Saul sees the Philistine army (1 Sam 28:5). Fear is what Jacob feels toward Esau (Gen 32:11) and Elijah toward Jezebel (1 Kgs 19:3). Surely that's not what Israel should feel toward God.

Of course, that depends on one's understanding of God. From a modern, perhaps Christian-inflected, perspective, the concepts "God is love" and "God is a source of fear" don't sit so easily beside each other. Or if the appropriate human posture toward God is one of *love* (as in, "You shall love the Lord your God"), then fear seems incompatible. Yet it isn't so clear that the Bible, or the world from which it emerged, shares these perspectives and postures.

Many of the references to the "fear of God" in the Bible are in the context of obedience, whether very frequently in Deuteronomy with regard to the laws ("Keep the commandments of the Lord your God by walking in his ways and by fearing him," Deut 8:6, NRSV), or, perhaps more famously in the narrative of Abraham's near-*sacrifice* of Isaac: "Do not lay your hand on the boy or do anything to him, for now I know that you fear God, since you have not withheld your son, your only son, from me" (Gen 22:12, NRSV).

Reverence, awe, respect—of course, these are all logical motivations for obedience and fit especially well with the depiction of God as monarch. And obedience may come from a love of the deity and from awe and reverence of God's mighty power. But the deity of the ancient world and our deity today are not the same. The God of ancient Israel, like virtually every other deity in the ancient Near East, was not just powerful—he was scary.

I have no interest in upholding the false "Old Testament god of wrath" notion. That said, Israel's god is hardly reluctant to impose severe punishments when angered, be it the flood in Genesis, the plagues in Numbers, or the destruction of the Temple in 2 Kings and Lamentations. Once there are laws to be obeyed—that is, basically after the book of Exodus—God's anger is almost always stoked by, unsurprisingly, disobedience. What's more, the laws themselves aren't given as a gift—they are imposed on Israel as Yahweh's due for having taken Israel out of Egypt. They are neither given in *love* nor received with *love*. And a not insignificant part of the motivation for obeying them is that failure to do so will result in utter destruction: "If you will not obey the Lord your God by diligently observing all his commandments and decrees, which I am commanding you today, then all these curses shall come upon you and overtake you" (Deut 28:15, NRSV).

Walking in God's ways, obeying God's laws, and fearing God—not in the abstract "revering" sense, but in the very material fear of loss of health, life, and land—were not distinct aspects of behavior but one and the same thing. Obedience demonstrated a healthy, appropriate fear of the divine being who could, and indeed would, destroy you for doing otherwise. The beginning of wisdom, indeed.

We—at least, most likely, those with access to this book—do not live in the state of material precarity that would have been familiar to nearly every ancient Israelite. Nor, for the most part, do we live in a state of wonder about the origins of our individual and collective ailments. What was once a real fear of a power beyond comprehension that was thought responsible for the many hardships of life has, over time, been softened into awe and respect for a power no less immense but somewhat more distant, and certainly less arbitrary. It is useful, though, to remember when we read the phrase "fear of the Lord" that it comes from a place of real fear—and that there may be those, perhaps less comfortable than we, who still know something of that fear.

§ 18

Kill (רצח, *ratzach*)

Thou shalt not kill.

Exodus 20:13 (KJV)

IF PUT ON the spot to name a single one of the Ten Commandments, chances are most people would come out with this one, the sixth, and probably even in the very language of the King James: "Thou shalt not kill." How much simpler could a commandment be? The classic interpretive problem, of course, is that it's almost too simple. "Kill" is a pretty vague word and prohibiting it would seem to be at odds with other parts of the Bible where killing isn't prohibited but actually required (see *ban*, for example). This interpretive difficulty, however, doesn't exist in the original Hebrew—but it does go back a pretty long way.

Just as English distinguishes between "murder" and "kill," so too does Biblical Hebrew. And the word used in the Ten Commandments is decidedly "murder": רצח. This word appears fewer than fifty times in the Bible and always in relatively limited circumstances: for what we would designate as murder—that is, the intentional taking of another person's life (as in 1 Kgs 21:19)—and for what we would call unintentional manslaughter (as in Num 35:11). Of course, you can make a law describing what to do in the case of unintentional manslaughter (which is what we have in the Bible, with the cities of refuge), but you can't really forbid it outright, it being unintentional and all. So what we have in the Ten Commandments can really refer only to intentional manslaughter: murder.

We have different words for "kill" and "murder" in English—so why does the King James use the generic term rather than the specific one? It's only partly the fault of the translators. The first culprit is Jerome, in his translation of the Bible into Latin, the Vulgate, back in the fourth century CE. The Septuagint, the Greek translation from the third century BCE, used the Greek equivalent of "murder," but Jerome chose the broader Latin term *occidere*, "kill." This wasn't really an error so much as a linguistic quirk: the Latin of Jerome's time didn't have a sharply defined word for "murder" as opposed to "kill." The term Jerome chose worked in both contexts equally.

But for the wide swath of Western Christianity that took Jerome's Vulgate as its primary biblical text, distinctions present in the Hebrew of the Ten Commandments and elsewhere in the Bible were obscured. There are multiple Hebrew words (הרג, המית, נכה, and others) for different types of killing: court-sanctioned death penalties, war, and divine punishment. For the ancient Israelite author and audience, however, the idea of prohibiting all killing would have been inconceivable. By using the same term for all of these, Jerome elided the original biblical distinctions: all killing was made equivalent. Now, though, judicial or military killing would appear to be both permissible, even legislated, and also prohibited by the Ten Commandments. The English translators of the King James emulated Jerome and repeated his error, but without the same linguistic excuse.

The ambiguity of the traditional Latin and English text has resulted in a wide variety of practical interpretations of this commandment. The overlap between those who claim to live according to biblical principles and those who support the death penalty in America, for example, is fairly well established. Martin Luther, in explaining this commandment, distinguished between individual killing, which is forbidden, and state-sanctioned killing, be it judicial or military, which is permitted. It is individuals who are not allowed to take decisions about life or death into their own hands. Such decisions are to be left to higher, and more collective, powers. This is, in fact, not far off from the original intent of the Ten Commandments (though Luther, like Jerome and the KJV, used a broad term for "kill" in his own influential translation of the Bible into German). In Catholicism, this commandment is invoked to explain the principle of the sanctity of life, which undergirds Catholic opposition to abortion as well as the death penalty. Yet it does not extend to killing in the context of a military conflict, which is permitted under the doctrine of "just war." On the furthest end of the spectrum, for those Christians who have been called "absolute pacifists" this commandment is the foundational principle, and the common rendering is essential. As the philosopher Bertrand Russell defined it, "The Commandment does not say you must only kill bad people, or only kill by due process of law, or only kill in defense of your country; it says, simply and unequivocally, 'Thou shalt not kill.'"

Language, tradition, and moral philosophy have all played a role in the translation and interpretation of this text as "kill," rather than "murder." It's a wonderful opportunity, then, to observe and recognize the extent to which our encounters with the biblical text in translation—whether ancient or modern—are shaped by forces entirely external to the Bible itself. This is no small matter: it's one of the Ten Commandments, and it's as basic a moral law as there is. In short, the most famous commandment of them all may also be, at least in its common rendering, one of the least well defined. Ironically, it is so only because translations from the Hebrew removed the specificity that was (and remains) present in the original text.

§ 19

Leprosy (צרעת, *tsara'at*)

Command the children of Israel, that they put out of the camp every leper.

Numbers 5:2 (KJV)

In modern medical terms, "leprosy" is a very specific diagnosis. It refers to what is known as Hansen's disease, an infection caused by Mycobacterium lepra. Unlike some other skin conditions, such as eczema or psoriasis, true leprosy is quite rare. It is, however, also quite (in)famous and widely feared and reviled, so much so that the noun "leper" has come to be used metaphorically for a social outcast. For this we have the Bible to thank. But the story is somewhat more complicated than that.

As scholars have long noted, the condition known as צרעת in the Bible is not, in fact, what we now call Hansen's disease. Thanks to the extensive ritual prescriptions in Leviticus 13–14, we have a detailed description of what skin conditions were given this label. Not only do they not conform to the modern definition of leprosy, they don't match any single contemporary medical diagnosis. In fact, we are probably mistaken in thinking of צרעת medically at all.

Texts about צרעת in the Bible come in two distinct forms. Across the Bible, various characters are struck with this skin disease as a form of divine punishment. Miriam in Numbers 12, Elisha's servant Gehazi in 2 Kings 5, the Judahite king Azariah (or Uzziah) in 2 Kings 15 (and 2 Chr 26). Divine punishments are not diagnosable—we are hardly inclined to try and figure out the modern medical equivalent of, say, any of the plagues that God sends against Israel. They are supernatural, not medical, in nature; they are caused by sin, not by bacteria.

In contrast to these narratives, we find in Leviticus 13–14 the mechanisms for recognizing צרעת and the sacrificial rites that are to be brought once it has disappeared. Here there is no sense of divine punishment: צרעת is merely one of the many conditions that cause *impurity*, along with others that occur naturally, such as seminal emissions, menstruation, and childbirth. Though these chapters do entail the inspection of the skin and the evaluation of whether the presenting symptoms do, in fact, constitute צרעת, the similarity to modern medical diagnostics ends there. For the one doing the inspecting and evaluating is not a doctor but a priest; what is decided is not what specific ailment the person in question suffers from but whether they are ritually pure or *impure*; and there is no course of treatment for the condition. In these chapters, צרעת is exclusively a ritual status.

Whether from divine punishment or naturally occurring impurity, one who suffers from צרעת is to be quarantined, isolated from others until the condition passes. This seems on its surface like a medical response for the purpose of preventing contagious infection. Fear of contagion certainly plays a role here. But those who are separated from the rest of Israel include not only those with skin disease, but also—in the same verse quoted in the header above—those who are *impure* from burying a corpse. That is to say, for the ancient Israelite author, what is at stake here is not medical infection but contagious ritual impurity.

Our medical diagnoses don't always map directly onto the ailments described in the Bible. And even if they did, it would still be a mistake to translate the ancient term with a modern medical one. We are accustomed to thinking within a medical system; ancient Israel was decidedly not. When we render their terms into our own, we risk importing our worldview back into theirs and thus obscuring the meaning that צרעת or other physical or mental conditions—Moses's "heavy tongue," Saul's "evil spirit," ritually impure genital flows, even common maladies such as blindness or deafness—might have had in ancient Israel.

If צרעת isn't modern-day leprosy, how did we end up translating it that way? In the Septuagint, the Greek translation of the Hebrew Bible, the term used to render צרעת was *lepra*. But like the Hebrew צרעת, the Greek *lepra* also had a rather broad meaning, describing a variety of skin conditions. It wouldn't be until the Middle Ages that this Greek term would be applied to the specific condition of what is now called Hansen's disease—and this was the term chosen precisely because it was known from the Bible. There is thus an ironic boomerang effect of sorts at play here: modern readers see a medically specific term in their Bibles because scholars centuries ago chose a generic biblical term to describe a specific illness. צרעת wasn't leprosy—and leprosy was never really צרעת.

Here, then, is a case where translation does more than just translate. If we think medically-diagnosed leprosy when we see "leprosy," we import a whole modern mode of thinking into the Bible. And at the same time, when we use "leprosy" as a metaphor for social ostracism we're exporting a notion from the Bible—be it divine punishment or ritual impurity—into our own context.

§ 20

Levite (לֵוִי, *levi*)

"What of your brother Aaron, the Levite?"

Exodus 4:14 (NRSV)

THE BIBLE TELLS us that the twelve tribes of Israel were each descended from one of Jacob's sons. Thus, a Judahite was descended from Judah; a Benjaminite from Benjamin; and a Levite from Levi. Biblical scholars and historians, however, tell us that the genetic kinship of the Israelite tribes is a fiction and that what made someone a Judahite is the fact that they lived in the territory known as Judah, while a Benjaminite lived in the territory called Benjamin. The biblical narrative supports this, in a sort of backward way: After all, the various tribes are largely indistinguishable until, after the conquest of Canaan, they each settle in their respective territories, the borders of which are very precisely defined for us (see Jos 14–19). Just as Israel as a whole isn't a nation until it has possession of a land, so too for each of the tribes.

All of which leaves us in something of a pickle when it comes to the Levites. Because, unlike all the other tribes, the Levites have no territory. There are a variety of explanations for why this is the case. According to Jacob's deathbed song in Genesis 49, Levi's descendants will receive no land inheritance because of the violence he perpetrated, along with Simeon, in the Dinah episode back in Genesis 34. In Joshua 18, we are told that the Levites have no territory among the Israelites because "the priesthood of the Lord is their heritage" (18:7, NRSV). In both cases there's an additional consideration at stake: Everyone knew, it seemed, that there were twelve tribes of Israel, but everyone also knew that Joseph, despite being one of Jacob's sons, was not a tribe or territory. Ephraim and Manasseh, Joseph's children according to the story, were the actual tribes and territories—and as a result you could count twelve Israelite tribes without including Levi at all. What we are seeing in the text is a conflict between a tradition (that Levi was one of the twelve sons of Jacob) and a reality on the ground (that Levi had no territory like the other tribes).

Then there is the question of where the Levites actually live. According to Numbers 8, the Levites are permanently assigned to the service of the sanctuary; they are designated as the servants of the priests. But it is clear from many other texts that, in fact, the Levites live all over Israel, not just at or around the sanctuary where the *ark* resides. Deuteronomy repeatedly assumes that there are Levites living in just about every Israelite town and even goes so far as to say that if a Levite would like to leave his town to go serve at the central sanctuary, he can (Deut 18:6–7). In Joshua 21, differently, the Levites are given specific towns—forty-eight of them, to be precise—taken from the territories of the other tribes. And in Judges 17, we read about "a young man of Bethlehem in Judah, of the clan of Judah," who, by any regular definition, would be a Judahite but who is said to be "a Levite residing there." (Bethlehem is not, it might be noted, one of the towns of Judah said to be assigned to the Levites in Joshua 21.)

The whole situation is rather messy. But there is a pretty good solution, even if it's one that doesn't quite comport with the biblical narrative we know and love.

"Levite" is probably best understood—at least in its origins—not as a tribal name at all. It is, more likely, a professional designation. (Linguistically, the Hebrew word, לוי, *levi*, is rather similar to another profession: נבאי, *nab'i*, "prophet.") A levite (lower case) would, originally, have been someone whose job was to serve in the sanctuary—that is, the local sanctuary in each Israelite town. This explains why Deuteronomy assumes that every town has levites in it. It would also explain why someone from the clan of Judah could also be a levite. And it also explains the oddity of Exodus 4:14, quoted above. It's not immediately clear why Yahweh would feel the need to describe Aaron, Moses's own brother, as a Levite when mentioning him to Moses. After all, if Levite is a tribal identifier, and Aaron and Moses are brothers, then, by definition, they would both be Levites, and saying so wouldn't be particularly enlightening. But if Aaron is a levite (lower case) by profession—and Moses, one then assumes, is not—suddenly the description makes much more sense.

What seems to have happened is that the profession, levite, became understood as a tribal designation—Levite. This may have taken place through a quirk of the language: the levites were occasionally referred to as בני לוי, *b'nei levi*, literally "sons of Levi," but more probably, "members of the category of levite" (see *sons of*). When taken literally, it was understood that there must have been an individual ancestor named Levi, and given the prominence of Levites early on in the biblical narrative—Aaron, for instance—it was thus assumed that this Levi was one of the sons of Jacob. But then there were too many tribes—so Levi was stripped of his inheritance, in various ways by various authors, and Ephraim and Manasseh could resume their proper place.

In the end, the precise mechanism by which levites became Levites may remain unknown. But it is useful for us as modern readers to recognize that such a shift did happen. For one thing, it helps make sense of some otherwise strange passages. It also has explanatory power, suggesting a rationale for the often-conflicting presentation of the Levites across biblical texts. The biblical authors were grappling—and not only here—with the same sort of confusion that we do: How do we deal with the tension between tradition and reality, between story and history?

§ 21

Hebrew (עברי, *'ivri*)

Thus says the Lord, the God of the Hebrews: Let my people go.
Exodus 9:1 (NRSV)

"HEBREW" IS USED today primarily to denote a language, whether it be the Modern Hebrew spoken in present-day Israel or the Biblical Hebrew of ancient times. Nowhere in the Hebrew Bible, however, ironically enough, is "Hebrew" used this way. When the language of ancient Israel is referred to, it is called "Judean" or "the language of Judah" (2 Kgs 18:26), which is sensible enough: Usually the language is named after the place in which it is spoken or vice versa. So in Judah, they speak Judean. There's nowhere called "Hebrew," so no one in the Bible speaks anything that they themselves would call "Hebrew."

Yet the word "Hebrew" appears in the Hebrew Bible, albeit relatively rarely: fewer than thirty-five times. It is always descriptive of a person or people, not a language. And, unsurprisingly, it is always used in reference to Israelites, as if the two words are synonyms. Which leaves us with a question: Why use the word "Hebrew" at all?

One of the notable features of "Hebrew" is not why it is used but by whom and in what circumstances. Ten times the term "Hebrew" is used by a non-Israelite to refer to Israelites: "My husband has brought among us a Hebrew to insult us!" says Potiphar's wife of Joseph (Gen 39:14, NRSV). Pharaoh demands the death of all boys born to "the Hebrew women" (Exod 1:16), and his daughter recognizes Moses as "one of the Hebrews' children" (Exod 2:6, NRSV). Not only the Egyptians but also the Philistines refer to Israelites as "Hebrew": "The Philistines said, 'The Hebrews must not make swords or spears for themselves'" (1 Sam 13:19, NRSV) and "The commanders of the Philistines said, 'What are these Hebrews doing here?'" (1 Sam 29:3, NRSV).

Another ten times "Hebrew" is used in almost the opposite way: by Israelites speaking to foreigners. Joseph declares to his Egyptian fellow prisoners that he was "stolen out of the land of the Hebrews" (Gen 40:15, NRSV). The midwives tell Pharaoh that "the Hebrew women are not like the Egyptian women" (Exod 1:19, NRSV). Moses's sister offers to get a nurse "from the Hebrew women" for Pharaoh's daughter (Exod 2:7, NRSV). Jonah tells the sailors on whose boat he is hiding, "I am a Hebrew" (Jon 1:9, NRSV). And repeatedly Moses, in speaking to Pharaoh, identifies Yahweh as "the God of the Hebrews," as in the quote above.

More than half of the occurrences of "Hebrew," then, are either from or to foreigners. In every case, the foreigner speaking or spoken to is of higher status. There is some sociological status-signaling going on here, it would seem. Perhaps a reasonable modern analogy is to the term "Yankee," which was used first by the British as a pejorative name for the American colonists and then during the Civil War era by the southern Confederates as a pejorative name for the northerners. Of course, often a pejorative term is adopted by its referent as a point of pride—the New York Yankees—and so it is no surprise that even Israelites occasionally use "Hebrew" to refer to themselves. When Saul's army defeats the Philistines, "Saul blew the trumpet throughout all the land, saying, 'Let the Hebrews hear!'" (1 Sam 13:3, NRSV).

What makes "Hebrew" potentially pejorative, however, is not immediately apparent. The usual etymology of the word links it to the name Eber (עבר), one of the early ancestors of Israel (Gen 10:21;

11:14–17). The root of the word is traditionally taken to be from עבר, "across," as in "the ones who dwell across the Jordan." Nothing there seems particularly insulting. In the nineteenth century, however, a new etymological contender entered the picture. As more material from ancient Mesopotamia and Egypt came to light, second-millennium BCE texts from across the ancient Near East referred to a previously unknown group: the Habiru.

The Habiru were not an ethnic group. They were, rather, a social group, and not a high-status one. In the second-millennium documents that attest to their presence, the Habiru are some combination of outlaws, mercenaries, and nomads, depending on the circumstances. They lived on the outskirts of society, occasionally of use but often more a nuisance. The term is even used as a pejorative designation for a ruler who rebels against his Egyptian overlord.

If we take all of that and then think about how "Hebrew" is used by foreigners in the Bible, a reasonable picture begins to emerge. For the Egyptian Pharaoh, what are the descendants of Jacob if not exactly this: nomadic nuisances who refuse to obey? One might, then, read "Hebrew" as no more than an insult. But we should also keep in mind that historically the Israelites probably were closer to the Habiru than the biblical narrative suggests. Israel emerges as a people and nascent nation in the twelfth century BCE, occupying scattered small settlements in the hill country of Canaan. It is likely that the early settlers of those sites were disaffected or marginalized people moving out of the major city centers of the coast and plains, perhaps under pressure from the newly arrived Philistines. These early Israelites may not have been identical with the earlier Habiru, but they certainly would have looked similar, especially to the major regional powers.

There is one set of texts in which "Hebrew" is used by Israelites about Israelites. In Exodus, in the laws of the Covenant Code, we read:

"When you buy a male Hebrew slave, he shall serve six years" (Exod 21:2, NRSV). Similarly in Deuteronomy: "If a member of your community, whether a Hebrew man or a Hebrew woman, is sold to you" (Deut 15:12, NRSV). And so too Jeremiah: "All should set free their Hebrew slaves" (Jer 34:9, NRSV). In all of the laws of the Bible, it is only here that we find the word "Hebrew" used: when referring to Israelites who are so poor that they have to sell themselves into slavery. In other words, even here "Hebrew" has a lower-class social signification.

"Hebrew" may have come to be synonymous with "Israelite," but it wasn't always. Given its likely origins and status marking, it is perhaps a word that we should be careful about, not only when we use it, if we do, but when we read it in the biblical text. Insider/outsider language, which "Hebrew" seems to be, can often be sensitive: Who uses it, and to whom, and in what situation, all matter.

§ 22

Sons of (בני, *b'nei*)

> *The sons of God saw the daughters of men that they were fair; and they took them wives of all which they chose.*
>
> Genesis 6:2 (KJV)

THE HEBREW WORD for son is *ben*, and the plural, sons, is *b'nei*. It's perhaps hard to see how such a basic word could be at all complicated or confusing. Then again, ask a non-native English speaker to explain the phrase "son of a gun" and it might become somewhat clearer. In Hebrew, as in English, to be the "son of" something does not always literally mean to be the male offspring of whatever it is. Recognizing this allows for a more nuanced understanding of certain texts, phrases, and expressions.

As it turns out, Hebrew uses "son/s of" in a manner similar to English. Sometimes, of course, it is literal: "These three were the sons of Noah" (Gen 9:19, NRSV), for example. Very often, however, it signifies not lineal genetic descent but membership in a category. A decent English version of this is the phrase "son of the south," which is to say, a southerner. Hebrew, remarkably, has the exact same expression, "son of the south"—but in Hebrew it comes out as a proper name, Benjamin: *ben-yamin*. There's no one named Yamin; *yamin* is the word for "south." That is, the tribe of Benjamin is basically "those people who live to the south"—in this case to the south of Ephraim and Manasseh, where the main bulk of Israel's early settlements were located.

The most common use of בני in this categorial sense is to refer to members of nations. The Hittites are the בני-*Het*: "the sons of Het," literally, but really just the Hittites. The Ammonites are the בני-*Ammon*. The Moabites are the בני-*Moab*, etc. And, of course, there are the בני-*Yisrael*. In this case, we can see how the biblical authors were conscious of and played with the dual functions of the word בני. At the very beginning of the book of Exodus, we get a list: "These are the names of the בני-*Yisrael* who came to Egypt with Jacob, each with his household" (Exod 1:1, NRSV), followed by, of course, the names of Jacob's literal male offspring. But just about as soon as that list is completed, we are told that "the בני-*Yisrael* were fruitful and prolific; they multiplied and grew exceedingly strong, so that the land was filled with them" (Exod 1:7, NRSV). In the conceptual space between those two verses is the transition from a small family, of Jacob's twelve sons, to a full-fledged nation. And that transition is marked by a shift in the use of the same phrase, בני-*Yisrael*, first to signify twelve individual children of Jacob and then to denote the people as a whole, the category of "Israelite."

Many readers of modern English Bibles won't even be aware when they see the word "Israelite" that what they're really reading is "sons of Israel." Even the King James has rendered it as "the children of Israel," which gives it a somewhat more general sense than "sons of Israel." Similarly, someone reading the NRSV or JPS translations of Deuteronomy 13:14 will find the word "scoundrel" and have no idea that the Hebrew is "sons of wickedness," בני-*b'liya'al*. But a reader of the King James would read in the same verse "sons of Belial," and likely imagine—as early interpreters seem also to have imagined—that there was some sort of demonic figure named "Belial." Here, then, is a case where not understanding how the Hebrew "sons of" construction works has led to confusion—and even to the creation of an entirely new figure in the biblical imagination.

The same is happening in the verse quoted in the epigraph above from Genesis. The KJV renders בני-*elohim* literally as "sons of God" as do virtually all modern English translations, with the notable exception of the JPS. The theological difficulty of such a translation would have been just as acute in ancient Israel at it feels to us today: Israel's god had no son—and, for later Christian readers, certainly no sons, plural. Here it is the non-literal sense that should be read: not "sons of God," but "members of the class of *elohim*"—that is, "divine beings," as the JPS correctly has it. Some readers might be taken aback even by the notion of divine beings other than God, but they are everywhere in the Hebrew Bible (see *angel* and *cherub*, e.g.). An equivalent example is to be found in the frequent phrase that Yahweh uses to address Ezekiel: בן-*adam*. "Son of man" is the classic translation, but what is meant is simply "mortal": member of the class of *adam*, humanity.

There is at least one feminine version of this construction. "Daughters of," בנות, usually means, literally, the female offspring of someone. But it is also used to denote the smaller villages surrounding a large town or city. These are not literally "daughters of" a place; they are, rather, individuals that belong to a larger collective.

Translations have muddied the dual use of בני, "sons of" (and its singular and feminine equivalents). Sometimes, as we have seen, they render it too literally, producing a variety of oddities, including in at least one case an entirely new demon. Other times, however, in translating the phrase appropriately in its collective sense, they have obscured the underlying Hebrew wording. It's a no-win situation, perhaps, which is why it is useful to know what it is that we're reading, whichever direction the translation happens to lean.

§ 23

Hell (שאול, *she'ol*)

> *The wicked shall be turned into hell, and all the nations that forget God.*
>
> Psalm 9:17 (KJV)

Hell as the post-mortem destination for the wicked is pretty standard stuff across many Christian denominations. Of course, the specifics differ widely: hell can be a physical location, beneath the earth or elsewhere, full of fire and eternal torture for those condemned there, or it can be a metaphorical state of distance and isolation from the divine. Whatever it's believed to be, however, the hell of Christianity, from antiquity to the present, is quite different from the Sheol of the Hebrew Bible and ancient Israel.

The biblical Sheol is most decidedly a physical place and is definitely located beneath the earth—it is an underworld like the Greek Hades. One always goes down to Sheol; it is often described as "the pit" (see, e.g., Isa 14:15). Famously, in Numbers 16, the rebels Dathan and Abiram are punished when the earth opens and swallows them: they "went down alive into Sheol" (Num 16:33). Job declares, "those who go down to Sheol do not come up" (Job 7:9, NRSV).

Unlike hell—but again like Hades—Sheol is not reserved for the wicked. It is the inevitable destination of everyone. "Who can live and never see death? Who can escape the power of Sheol?" (Ps 89:48,

NRSV). "In death there is no remembrance of you; in Sheol who can give you praise?" (Ps 6:5, NRSV). "Shall I ransom them from the power of Sheol? Shall I redeem them from death?" (Hos 13:14, NRSV). In all these verses and others like them, "Sheol" and "death" are one and the same. Sheol is simply the place where the dead go.

There's nothing inherently bad about Sheol. What matters isn't whether one ends up there—everyone does—but rather the manner in which one ends up there. One certainly would not want to go down to Sheol alive, like Dathan and Abiram. Nor would one want to be prematurely led there, as Proverbs warns of the "loose woman" who embodies a lack of wisdom: "her steps follow the path to Sheol" (Prov 5:5, NRSV). Many of the psalms employ the image of Sheol to symbolize sorrow: "My soul is full of troubles, and my life draws near to Sheol" (Ps 88:3, NRSV). Though Sheol is an unavoidable destination, like death it is hardly a desirable one. If one has to go there, better to go having lived a full and pleasant life rather than one "full of troubles."

Here, too, we find a significant difference from the later concept of hell; not only do good people go to Sheol as well as bad, but it is entirely possible to go down to Sheol pleasantly: "They spend their days in prosperity, and in peace they go down to Sheol" (Job 21:13, NRSV). Here one could hardly translate Sheol as "hell"—and, notably, the KJV here, and in similar settings, renders Sheol as "the grave." Which is, in a sense, an acknowledgment that where "hell" is used it is an imposition, an effort to insert a Christian theological position into the Hebrew Bible.

At the end of a long and happy life, death, in its proper time, is not unwelcome. One may go to Sheol content. This is the fate one wishes on those one loves. Alternatively, one wishes the opposite on one's enemies: "Do not let his gray head go down to Sheol in peace," David instructs Solomon about Joab (1 Kgs 2:6, NRSV). Or, more directly, "You must bring his gray head down with blood to Sheol," about Shimei (1 Kgs

2:9, NRSV). Jacob is worried that, should harm come to Benjamin, his sons will "bring down my gray hairs with sorrow to Sheol" (Gen 42:38, NRSV).

Sheol isn't a place of torture—after all, there are good people down there too. The biblical conception of the afterlife is one of, well, nothing: "There is no work or thought or knowledge or wisdom in Sheol, to which you are going" (Eccl 9:10, NRSV). In that sense, it could be thought of as better than a life of pain. At least, this is what Job suggests: "Oh that you would hide me in Sheol, that you would conceal me until your wrath is past" (Job 14:13, NRSV). It's hard to imagine anyone saying the same about hell.

Where there seems to be some internal debate in the Bible regarding Sheol, it has to do with the permanence of one's time there. Which is, perhaps, simply to say that the Bible is inconsistent on the question of post-mortem resurrection. "As the cloud fades and vanishes, so those who go down to Sheol do not come up" (Job 7:9, NRSV). Permanent, then. On the other hand: "Yahweh kills and brings to life; he brings down to Sheol and raises up" (1 Sam 2:6, NRSV). Not so permanent! A reader looking for resurrection in the text might also find it with some frequency in the psalms: "O Lord, you brought up my soul from Sheol" (Ps 30:3, NRSV). "God will ransom my soul from the power of Sheol" (Ps 49:15, NRSV). "You have delivered my soul from the depths of Sheol" (Ps 86:13, NRSV). Of course, these only work as references to resurrection if they're understood to be spoken by someone who has, in fact, already been resurrected. But as an allusion to the possibility, they do the trick.

What we're really seeing here, though, is Sheol as metaphor—and here is where it does overlap somewhat with hell. Just as we might say, in times of distress, that life has become a living hell, so too the speakers of the psalms declare their misery in terms of Sheol: "The snares of death encompassed me; the pangs of Sheol laid hold on me; I suffered distress and anguish" (Ps 116:3, NRSV). Release from that misery is like being brought back from the dead—like being raised from Sheol, from darkness to light, from nothingness into the fullness of being.

Hell is, fundamentally, a divisive concept: some are there, physically or metaphorically, while others are in a better place. The biblical Sheol offers another vision: of a common fate for all, although with different paths to arrive there.

§ 24

Heart (לבב/לב, *lev, levav*)

Keep these words that I am commanding you this day in your heart.
Deuteronomy 6:6 (NRSV)

THE DIFFERENCE BETWEEN the mind and the heart is a standard feature of our sense of self. The mind is cold and calculating; the heart is warm and sensitive. The mind overflows with ideas; the heart overflows with love. The mind is the seat of cognition; the heart is the seat of emotion. Consciously or not, we bring this division of the self to our reading of the Bible. When we read that the words of the law are to be kept "in your heart," as in the quote above, we understand it to mean something more, something deeper, than just remembered or kept "in mind." There is, of course, nothing objective about this. It is entirely a product of cultural context—specifically, Western culture. In other settings—among them ancient Israel—there is no such clear distinction between the heart and the mind. In fact, there is no word in Biblical Hebrew for "mind" or "brain." When you read the word "mind" in your English Bible, it is most often translating the word לב or לבב: that is, "heart."

Many of the qualities that we associate with the mind belong, in the Bible, to the heart. First and foremost, the heart is the seat of cognition. Even in the very first occurrence of the word in the Bible this is evident: "The Lord saw that the wickedness of humankind was great in the earth, and that every inclination of the thoughts of their hearts was only evil continually" (Gen 6:5, NRSV). The "thoughts of their hearts"—or, for another example, Deuteronomy 29:3 [English 29:4, NRSV]: "But to this day the Lord has not given you a לב to understand." Or, "their eyes are shut so that they cannot see, and their לבs as well, so that they cannot understand" (Isa 44:18, NRSV). The heart is the seat of intelligence and wisdom, as in Ezekiel 28:4–6. It is where understanding takes place: "Give me understanding, that I may keep your law and observe it with my whole heart" (Ps 119:34, NRSV).

The heart is where the will lives, where one's inclinations are located. Plans are made there. This is what is meant by the recurring phrase "hardening the heart," most famous from the story of the plagues in Exodus. When Yahweh hardens Pharaoh's heart, he prevents the Egyptian king from changing his mind. The signs and wonders that Moses and Aaron do before Pharaoh would, under normal circumstances, convince him to let Israel go; but, as Yahweh says, "I will harden Pharaoh's heart that I might multiply my signs and wonders in the land of Egypt" (Exod 7:3). It isn't about stiffening Pharaoh's resolve; it is about fixing his intentions, preventing mental flexibility. We might, in this light, also think about the famous description of David: "the Lord has sought out a man after his own heart" (1 Sam 13:14, NRSV). With a Western notion of the heart, this might mean all sorts of things; in the Hebrew, it might well mean simply "a man who has the same inclinations as Yahweh."

For us, speaking "from the heart" implies a greater truthfulness, a deeper honesty. In the Bible, all speech is from the heart. It is the organ from which speech originates (eventually moving up through the throat, mouth, and lips). "My heart overflows with a goodly theme; I address my verses to the king" (Ps 45:1, NRSV). "With my whole heart I cry" (Ps 119:145, NRSV). "Surely they will teach you and tell you, speaking out of their לב" (Job 8:10, JPS). Not only does speech emerge from the heart, it is also stored there: "You shall put these words of mine in your heart" (Deut 11:18, NRSV); "All the words that I shall speak to you receive in your heart" (Ezek 3:10). When we read in our English translations the phrase "said to himself"—as in "Abraham fell on his face and laughed, and said to himself" (Gen 17:17, NRSV)—this is a translation of the Hebrew "said in his heart." That is, the heart is acting as both origin and destination of speech.

Thinking, understanding, wisdom, inclination, planning, speech—these are, to our minds (pun intended) mental qualities. Yet in the Bible they belong exclusively to the heart. So too imagination: "This is how you shall know that Yahweh has sent me to do all these works; it has not been from my לב," Moses says to the rebellious Dathan and Abiram (Num 16:28). "I'm not making it up," Moses is saying—it isn't "from my heart." It is where memories reside: "In those days, says Yahweh, they shall no longer say, 'The ark of the covenant of Yahweh.' It shall not arise upon the heart, or be remembered, or missed" (Jer 3:16)—the NRSV translates "arise upon the heart" as "come to mind."

The biblical heart encompasses those qualities we attribute to the mind—but it also, of course, contains those we think of as belonging to the heart. It is where courage is located (Jos 2:11), and desire (Ps 37:4), and emotion: "Hannah, why do you weep? Why do you not eat? Why is your heart sad?" (1 Sam 1:8, NRSV). The heart is not just cognition; it is not just emotion. It is all of that which we think of as being internal: "the Lord does not see as mortals see; they look on the outward appearance, but the Lord looks on the heart" (1 Sam 16:7, NRSV).

How we think about the heart is a signature of our cultural context. And how we translate it is, too. Most modern translations translate לב or לבב in accordance with our modern Western notions. So when emotions are involved, or a sense of something deeper than mere understanding or intellect, "heart" is used. And when it seems to relate to a mental process, it becomes "mind." But we might consider an alternative. Rather than reinforce the modern Western dichotomy of heart and head, a translation attempting to represent biblical concepts and values might, in fact, simply say "heart" every time. It would perhaps sound strange at points, but that might be a fine thing. It might expand our sense of what the heart is or can be. It might allow us to see, in our own Bibles, a different way of understanding ourselves.

§ 25

Stranger (גר, *ger*)

> *The stranger who resides with you shall be to you as one of your citizens; you shall love him as yourself, for you were strangers in the land of Egypt.*
>
> Leviticus 19:34 (JPS)

"STRANGER" IS, TO put it simply, a strange word—at least as it's used in most Bible translations. A stranger, at least in its common usage, is someone unknown—but the biblical stranger can be very familiar indeed. A stranger might live in the same town as you—but the biblical stranger is explicitly not a citizen, as the quote above makes clear. Stranger is an interpersonal term of relation—but in the Bible it is, rather, international: "you were strangers in the land of Egypt," as in the epigraph above. All that to say: "stranger" does virtually none of the communicative work that we might want from a useful translation.

Scholars often define גר with a technical modern term: "resident alien." It's unwieldy, and feels anachronistic in the biblical text, to be sure. But it also captures important aspects of the biblical גר. The גר is not a citizen but is also not a foreigner, for which there is a different Hebrew word (נכרי, *nokhri*). The גר is an alien—in the technical diplomatic sense, a non-citizen—but one that chooses to reside in Israel. The choice is important: one cannot be forced to be a גר. A foreigner captured in battle and taken as a slave is not a גר, and cannot ever be.

Israel was a "stranger" in Egypt not because it was enslaved there but because Jacob and his descendants voluntarily decided to settle there in the face of famine.

While in theory one could choose to be a resident alien in Israel simply for fun, as it were, the paradigmatic גר is Israel itself, in Egypt; or Abraham in Egypt, or Jacob in Gerar: individuals and families escaping hardship in search of a better life. "We have come to be a גר in this land, for there is no pasture for your servants' flocks, the famine being severe in the land of Canaan," Joseph's brothers tell Pharaoh in Genesis 47:4. The stranger is in need: they rely on the kindness of the people among whom they seek to dwell.

The laws of Deuteronomy repeatedly include the stranger in the list of vulnerable members of the population, along with widows, orphans, and *Levites*. "Cursed be anyone who deprives the גר, the orphan, and the widow of justice" (Deut 27:19, NRSV). Widows, orphans, and Levites are Israelites and deserve protection as members of Israelite society; the stranger, by contrast, is a protected class because of the broad cross-cultural ancient Near Eastern commitment to hospitality. It is this commitment that the residents of Sodom violate: "This fellow came here as a גר . . . now we will deal worse with you than with them" (Gen 19:9, NRSV). The stories of Sodom and the Exodus are perhaps the two most prominent examples of the poor treatment of the stranger, and both are used as examples of what not to do—the Exodus repeatedly, as in the verse quoted above, and Sodom in Ezekiel: "This was the sin of your sister, Sodom: arrogance! . . . She did not support the poor and the needy" (Ezek 16:49, JPS). Biblical גר is, fundamentally, a socio-economic status.

The stranger was not only vulnerable and protected but also actively welcomed. A גר could offer *sacrifices* at the temple and celebrate the festivals (Lev 17:8; 22:18; Num 15:14). Even the most quintessentially

Israelite rituals were available to the stranger: the Passover offering, for example, which is explicitly forbidden to foreigners (Exod 12:43) but which is just as explicitly permitted to the גר (Exod 12:48; admittedly, the גר has to undergo circumcision before bringing the Passover offering, but it's still something!). With these rights, however, came responsibilities: the stranger is bound to the laws of the land. "You shall have one law for the גר and for the citizen" (Lev 24:22, NRSV). Thus the stranger is, like the native Israelite, forbidden to have any leaven in their house during the week of unleavened bread (Exod 12:19); to work on Yom Kippur (Lev 16:29); to consume blood (Lev 17:10); to offer their offspring to Molech (Lev 20:2); to blaspheme (Lev 24:16); or to affront Yahweh (Num 15:30). The stranger even contracts impurity just like an Israelite (Lev 17:15).

The stranger, then, has virtually all the rights and responsibilities of an Israelite. It is not surprising, perhaps, that in Jewish tradition, the word גר came to mean "convert." In the biblical period, being an Israelite meant, first and foremost, living and owning land (going back generations) in the territory of Israel. In the diaspora after the destruction of the second temple in 70 CE, however, Jewish identity was no longer tied to land, but to religious practice. To be a גר in that context was to take on the religious obligations of Judaism—to convert. Judaism, as is well known, is not a religion that seeks out converts, and this too goes back to the biblical גר. One chooses to live in Israel or to become Jewish. And there is one law for both the גר and the citizen.

Today, the concept of "welcoming the stranger" is often raised in discourse around immigration. To what extent are we individually or communally responsible for caring for and protecting those who have chosen to live among us? Many features of the modern immigrant overlap with the biblical גר, not least of all the common desire to escape famine or other hardship in one's native country, to seek a better life.

What is perhaps often forgotten, especially by those of us who live in the global north, is that the biblical laws and customs regarding the גר weren't meant to be unidirectional. Israelites were expected to care for the stranger because it was understood that they would someday be strangers themselves, as they were in Egypt long ago, and as they would indeed be again, for nearly two thousand years. What the word "stranger" ultimately fails to capture is the recognition that this is not really an issue of us as opposed to them; we are all strangers.

Intermezzo

§ 26

Behold (הנה, *hinneh*)

> *And the angel of the Lord appeared to him in a flame of fire out of the midst of a bush: and he looked, and, behold, the bush burned with fire, and the bush was not consumed.*
>
> Exodus 3:2 (KJV)

Is any word more biblical than "behold"? Aside from a good old-fashioned "thee" or "thou" or "thy," nothing sounds quite so much like Bible-talk than "behold." As so often, we have the KJV to thank. The translators took one of the most common Hebrew words, הנה, which occurs over a thousand times, and rendered it as "behold" almost everywhere. In some places it's the equally King Jamesian "lo." What the King James never has, it turns out, is "lo and behold." Where the word הנה appears twice in a verse, it's "behold . . . and lo," as in Genesis 37:7, for example.

From a pure translation perspective, it's not really advisable to use words that aren't current in the target language. No one today says "Behold!" basically ever, so it's a little odd to find it so often in an English Bible. Of course, we expect it when it comes to the King James, which was translated to sound intentionally old-fashioned ("thee," "thou," "saidst," etc.—that's not actually how people spoke in the 1600s). When we remove the "biblical-ese" from our minds, we find that this little word, הנה, in fact has two distinct uses, and that "behold," or even a more modern equivalent like "look," doesn't quite capture what it's up to.

The first use of הנה has almost nothing at all to do with "behold." When the word appears in front of a participle—roughly the equivalent of the present tense in Biblical Hebrew—it signals that what follows is not happening right now but will happen very soon, sometimes even immediately. It is, in short, the Hebrew equivalent of the English "about to." For example, in Genesis 48:21, "Israel said unto Joseph, Behold, I die: but God shall be with you," as the KJV has it. "Behold" is הנה. "I die" is the participle of מות, "to die." The better translation would be, "Israel said to Joseph, 'I am about to die; but God shall be with you.'" Or in Genesis 6:17 (KJV): "Behold, I, even I, do bring a flood of waters upon the earth." Behold, I do bring? This is in God's instructions to Noah, where he tells him to get the animals and all that. Not "Behold, I do bring," but "I am about to bring." Saying "behold" in these situations makes it sound like there's something to actually behold—but there isn't, at least not yet. This is the הנה that, along with the participle, marks near-future action. About to.

Now, the other use of הנה is certainly closer to "behold," or at least to some modern equivalent, like "look." It's what we call a presentative particle, a word that draws our attention to something. So we find examples like Genesis 20:15 (KJV): "Abimelech said, Behold, my land is before thee: dwell where it pleaseth thee." Or Exodus 1:9 (KJV): "He said unto his people, Behold, the people of the children of Israel are more and mightier than we." Even in these cases, "behold" feels somewhat off, insofar as there's nothing tangible to really look at. It's almost more of a "hey." And sometimes when characters use the word הנה, it's not even quite a "hey," but more equivalent to a finger point. Genesis 18:9 (KJV): "They said unto him, Where is Sarah thy wife? And he said, Behold, in the tent." Or Genesis 37:19 (KJV): "They said one to another, Behold, this dreamer cometh."

But often when we see הנה, it isn't a character speaking at all. It's the narrator—and it makes little sense for the narrator to be saying "behold," in the imperative, as if commanding the reader to look at something occurring in the world of the story. If we've become accustomed to it because it sounds biblical, putting it into more modern English should defamiliarize it. "When her days to be delivered were fulfilled, look, there were twins in her womb" (Gen 25:24). It's really quite strange.

And yet, as strange as it seems to the ear and eye, this "behold" or "look" isn't so far off from what the word הנה would have signaled to the ancient author and reader (or better, listener). The best way to think about it is as a bit of direction, like in a film script. What הנה does, practically speaking, is turn our attention from whatever it was on before to something new that has entered the scene. Often it comes precisely when a character is actually seeing something for the first time, as in Genesis 22:13: "Abraham lifted his eyes, and looked, and הנה"—and just as the particle introduces the thing that Abraham is seeing in the story, so too it is introducing to us, the reader, the thing that has just entered the scene (in this case, the ram that will substitute for Isaac). It's easy to imagine this on screen: we're looking at Abraham as he speaks with the angel, but then as Abraham lifts his eyes and sees the ram, so the camera pivots from Abraham to the ram, and we see it, too. In essence, we see what Abraham is seeing; we get to identify with Abraham in that moment of recognition. The same is happening in, say, Genesis 28:12: "He had a dream: הנה a stairway was set on the ground and its top reached the sky, and הנה angels of God were ascending and descending on it." הנה draws our attention, like that of the characters in the story, to what is new, fascinating, wonderful.

"Behold" may be old-fashioned, and using a modern equivalent is still pretty awkward. As it turns out, הנה is hard to translate—and many modern translations just ignore it. But it's good to know when it's there, because it brings us into the world of the text unlike almost anything else.

III

Words That Connect God and People

§ 27

Love (אהב, *'ahav*)

You shall love the Lord your god.

Deuteronomy 6:5 (NRSV, JPS)

"LOVE" IS A tricky term, and a minefield for translation, on multiple levels. In English, it is a broad term, encompassing a range of overlapping concepts, from romance ("I love you") to desire ("I would love to") to tenderness ("I love my cat") to enjoyment ("I love sushi"). When we encounter it in the Bible, it isn't always perfectly clear which of these nuances is primary. Complicating the picture further is the recognition that the ideas we associate with the word "love" may not be the same ideas that are associated with it in other cultures, from other times and places. The Hebrew word אהב may be commonly translated as "love," but it has its own range of connotations and uses.

At its root, אהב has to do with preference. More than once in biblical poetry we find it used in parallel with the word "choose," as in Isaiah 41:8: "Jacob, whom I have chosen, the offspring of Abraham, my beloved." God's relation to Israel's patriarchs is often couched in this sort of language: "Because he loved your ancestors, he chose their offspring after them . . ." (Deut 4:37, NRSV). Expressed here is not romance, clearly, or even affection in a modern sense of "love." Rather, this is, as the text makes clear, about selection: of all the peoples of the earth, Yahweh chose Abraham and his descendants as his own people.

This is not to say that אהב never has romantic or affectionate connotations. "Saul's daughter Michal loved David" (1 Sam 18:20, NRSV), for example, may well be just that. Even here, however, we must be cautious about assuming that romance now is like romance then. When we imagine the past as being just like the present, we're probably making some serious assumptions about the universality of our own experience.

Quite often, even in marital relationships, the word "love" still hews closer to the notion of preference than it does to romance. Deuteronomy 21 ensures that a man with two wives treats their children even-handedly, even if he "loves" one wife and "hates" the other. "Prefers" is a superior rendering to "loves" here. So too in the story that exemplifies this situation: Jacob "loved Rachel more than Leah" (Gen 29:30). Better: "Jacob preferred Rachel to Leah."

The word אהב is used most often in this sort of context: where there are multiple potential figures, and one is lifted above the others: "Take your son, your beloved one, Isaac" (Gen 22:2). "Beloved" is used here not in some abstract sense of affection, but rather in the sense of "preferred," with regard to Ishmael: "Isaac loved Esau, but Rebekah loved Jacob" (Gen 25:28). Again, "Isaac preferred Esau, but Rebekah preferred Jacob." And again, "Israel loved Joseph best of all his sons" (Gen 37:3, JPS)—or, more to the point, "Israel preferred Joseph to all his (other) sons."

And, though this is somewhat harder to reckon with from our modern theological position, it is this notion of preference of one possibility among many that underlies perhaps the most famous use of the word "love" in the Bible: "You shall love the Lord your god" (Deut 6:5). For all the authentic heartfelt emotion that has been attached to this command in the history of its interpretation, what was originally meant here was simpler: you shall prefer Yahweh, the god of Israel, to any other deities out there. Deuteronomy was written before Israel was properly monotheistic. Other gods were understood to exist—every nation had one. Deuteronomy's overarching message, crystallized here, is that Israel is obligated to follow Yahweh and none other.

The formula used here would have been familiar to the educated reader in seventh-century BCE Judah, when Deuteronomy was written. "Love" is a technical term from the lexicon of international diplomacy. In multiple texts from the ancient Near East, stretching back a full millennium before the seventh century BCE, treaties and other diplomatic texts use the word "love" to denote the loyalty that the inferior party is obligated to demonstrate toward the superior. Those who "love" are the king's or emperor's subjects; those who oppose him are those who "hate." This is the very language used in the Ten Commandments: God will punish the third and fourth generation of those who "hate" him but will be steadfast to the thousandth generation of those who "love" him and keep his commandments (Deut 5:9–10). Just as the ancient Near Eastern ruler is concerned that his subjects might give their allegiance to another king, so too Yahweh is concerned that Israel might give their obedience to another deity. Thus the command: you shall love—really, you shall prefer, indeed, you shall be loyal to—Yahweh your god.

When we encounter the word "love" in the Bible, we naturally fill it with all our modern associations with the term, as have interpreters throughout the ages. Yet the ancient Israelite authors and audience would have heard an entirely different set of resonances. Both are part of the biblical text: what it meant, and what it means to us.

§ 28

Atone (כפר, *kipper*)

> *This shall be an everlasting statute unto you, to make an atonement for the children of Israel for all their sins once a year.*
>
> Leviticus 16:34 (KJV)

PERHAPS THE LEAST well understood part of the Hebrew Bible is the mass of sacrificial laws that occupy much of the book of Leviticus. This is in no small part because the entire system is totally foreign to us today: We do not offer bloody animal *sacrifices*, and, indeed, no one has (at least not in the biblical mode) for over two thousand years. At the center of the levitical system, however, at least in its common translation, is a concept that has endured: atonement.

Atonement is generally understood to be the making of amends, some sort of reparation or payment for a past wrong. And that is the context in which we find it in the Bible. When one commits an unintentional sin—it is, biblically speaking, impossible to atone for an intentional sin—one brings a specific offering to the sanctuary, and through sacrificing that offering the priest effects atonement on the offeror's behalf. It seems simple enough, and reasonably recognizable. Even if we no longer bring animal *sacrifices*, we still look to make amends for our sins, and for many this still requires the intermediation of a member of the clergy.

Yet this seemingly straightforward exchange is a far cry from the original idea—and the distance between what atonement was, and what it came to be, contains a major theological shift.

In its earliest form, the sacrificial system in Leviticus was devised for a single purpose: to maintain the dwelling-place of the deity, the sanctuary. At the end of Exodus, Moses and the Israelites construct the Tabernacle, where God will literally dwell in their midst. The laws that follow, in Leviticus 1–16, are about the maintenance of that divine dwelling. Specifically, they are about keeping it clean: free of the (unintentional) sins and the various impurities that the Israelite people generate. These sins and impurities, in this system, are drawn to and adhere to the sacred space. Too much of them, and there is the risk that God will leave his sullied home and, thus, remove his protective presence from Israel.

What prevents such a terrible outcome are the *sacrifices*. In particular, there are those *sacrifices* that are designed to remove the accumulated sins and impurities from the sanctuary. And it is here, with this idea of removal, that the word כפר is used. The Hebrew comes from a Mesopotamian term, ***kuppuru***, which means "purge," and that is precisely what it does here as well. What makes the sacrifice work is the animal's blood, which is applied to the sacred space through daubing and sprinkling and which acts as a sort of ritual detergent, purging the sancta of sins and impurities. This is why a priest is needed: Lay Israelites cannot perform sacrificial rites or access the affected parts of the sanctuary. It is the blood that purges; and, crucially, it is the sanctuary that is the object of the purging.

There is no moral valence to this process. The sin in question is unintentional; the impurity is usually unavoidable and sometimes even desirable (as in the impurity caused by childbirth or by burying one's family member; see *impure*). The one who commits the sin, or generates the impurity, is not at fault for doing so—they are, however, responsible for its removal from the sanctuary. As long as they provide the offering to perform the cleansing ritual, they are free of guilt. It is only if they fail to do so that they begin to get into trouble. The easy analogy is to the child who spills a glass of milk on the floor. Accidents happen—but if the child refuses to clean up the mess, not only will the milk start to spoil and smell worse, but the parent will become angry. That's the sacrificial system in Leviticus. To כפר is not to gain forgiveness; it is to clean up one's mess and thus restore things to the way they were.

Fundamentally, the כפר process was designed not for the benefit of the individual offeror but rather for that of the entire community. If everyone simply cleans up their own mess, then the deity will remain in the midst of the whole people, with the benefits that flow to all. The original sacrifices in Leviticus were not about making the individual whole but about keeping the collective protected.

What happens to such a system when the sanctuary around which it was oriented is destroyed? What happens when the concern for maintaining the present situation turns to a focus on an eschatological vision of future restoration? What once was collective becomes individual; what was once about preservation becomes about salvation. Purging, of the sanctuary, became understood as atoning, by and for the individual. It was through this ritual act—even in the imagination, as it was no longer performed in reality—that one could be forgiven of sins, be cleansed of impurities, and maintain one's standing before God.

This was a shift that happened already within Judaism but was accelerated by Christian theology, with its emphasis on the eschatological salvation of the individual. Atonement was, and largely remains, about the status of one's soul. But the purgation that כפר originally represented was not.

This is thus a wonderful example of a term whose meaning has changed to fit its social contexts. The shift from purgation to atonement is nothing more than the common, longstanding effort to make the Bible, even in its most technical and time-bound details, relevant to the living community of believers. It is also a fine opportunity to step back and recognize that there was meaning, and value, in the term's now-defunct use. Atonement, though an individual concern now, carries with it still the idea of communal benefit. What do we atone for—and for whose benefit?

§ 29

Law (תורה, *torah*)

Moses wrote down this law.

Deuteronomy 31:9 (NRSV)

THE VERSE QUOTED above is the primary source for the traditional claim that Moses was the author of the Pentateuch, the first five books of the Bible. And why not? The Hebrew word תורה, still in common use in English as "Torah," has been used in Judaism and beyond for the Pentateuch since antiquity. So "Moses wrote down this Torah" would seem to be fairly clear. Of course, things are rarely so simple.

At its root, תורה comes from the verb *yarah*, meaning "teach." A תורה is thus a teaching (or instruction), as it is sometimes translated. This is certainly a fitting description of the Pentateuch, consisting, as it does, primarily of laws and rituals for Israel to follow. But it can also refer to other texts or to non-textual instructions. The history of Moses's authorship of the Pentateuch is inextricably intertwined with the gradual shift in the meaning of תורה, a shift that we can see at work in the Bible itself.

There is plenty of evidence that תורה was used in a variety of ways before there was a Torah or Pentateuch. In Genesis, before any formal laws have been given, God describes Abraham as having kept "my commandments, my laws, and my תורהs"—all three terms used, essentially interchangeably, in reference to Abraham's obedience to God's various instructions over his lifetime. In Exodus 16, God tests the Israelites by giving them instructions about how and when to collect manna; these very specific commands are also referred to as תורה. God need not be the origin of a תורה: "My son, keep your father's commandment; do not forsake your mother's תורה," we read in Proverbs 6:20 (JPS).

Individual laws are called תורה. Upon giving the law for who can eat the *Passover* offering, God says to Moses, "There shall be one תורה for the citizen and the stranger who dwells among you" (Exod 12:49, JPS). In Leviticus, each type of sacrifice has its own ritual procedures: "This is the תורה of the burnt offering" (Lev 6:2); "This is the תורה of the meal offering" (6:7); "This is the תורה of the sin offering" (6:18); "This is the תורה of the guilt offering" (7:1); "This is the תורה of the sacrifice of well-being" (7:11); "This is the תורה for the leper" (14:2), etc.

Each of those rituals was its own תורה, but the word also came to be used for a collection of laws (much as the English "law" can refer to both single laws and an entire body of legal tradition). This is how it is used, notably, in Deuteronomy. In his final speeches to Israel, Moses sets before them a תורה, referred to always in Deuteronomy as "this Torah." The term here is self-referential: Deuteronomy doesn't mean the entire Pentateuch (which didn't exist when Deuteronomy was written), but itself alone. The laws are introduced with the title: "This is the תורה that Moses set before the Israelites" (Deut 4:44). And thus Moses's speech ends as well: "Take to heart all the words with which I have warned you this day. Enjoin them upon your children, that they may observe faithfully all the terms of this תורה" (Deut 32:46, JPS). The תורה, for Deuteronomy, is the contents of Moses's speech to Israel "this day," that is, on the last day of Moses's life; that is, in Deuteronomy.

In the books that immediately follow Deuteronomy, we have further references to תורה—not, still, to the entire Pentateuch, but seemingly still only to Deuteronomy. Here it is not "this Torah" that is referred to, but "the Torah of Moses," and often with language and ideas taken from Deuteronomy: "the תורה that Moses the servant of the Lord enjoined upon you, to love the Lord your god and to walk in all his ways, and to keep his commandments and hold fast to him, and to serve him with all your heart and soul" (Josh 22:5, JPS). The title "Torah of Moses" has caused its fair share of confusion—it meant not "the Torah written by Moses," but "the Torah given by Moses," or, as in the previously cited verse, "the Torah enjoined upon you by Moses." "Of" is a slippery word: we might hear "Torah of Moses" or "Psalms of David" as indicating authorship, but we wouldn't think the same about "the book of Ruth," for example.

It is not until nearly the end of the biblical period, in the books of Ezra, Nehemiah, and Chronicles, that תורה is used to denote something close to what we now think of as the complete Pentateuch. In Nehemiah 8, we find the story of Ezra reciting the תורה to Israel—reciting not just Deuteronomy, but seemingly the whole thing, or at least parts also from Leviticus. In Chronicles, kings and priests act "according to the תורה of Moses," fulfilling laws found scattered throughout the Pentateuch. It is only from this point onward that תורה comes to have its present-day meaning of "Torah."

Over two thousand years of tradition have understood תורה to refer to the canonical Pentateuch, even when it didn't always make sense: The classical rabbis claimed that Abraham knew the entire Torah even before God gave it to Moses at Sinai. Recognizing the history of the word's development, however, opens a variety of interesting doors. We might take up a verse such as Psalm 19:8—"The תורה of Yahweh is perfect, renewing life"—and ask what it would mean to read that not as "the Torah," but as "instruction, teaching, way, path." When Isaiah says "תורה shall come forth from Zion" (Isa 2:3), what might that mean? And in the broadest sense, we might consider the possibility that even within the Hebrew Bible, as much as we think of it as "law" or even "Law," what is set forth as guidance and instruction need not be legal, or legalistic; need not be formal; need not even be from God.

§ 30

Lovingkindness (חסד, *hesed*)

> *Know therefore that the Lord is your God, he is God, the faithful God, who keeps his covenant and his lovingkindness to a thousandth generation with those who love him and keep his commandments.*
>
> Deuteronomy 7:9 (NASB)

"LOVINGKINDNESS" IS . . . not a real word. (It is, evidently, the name for a contemporary meditation practice. Still.) The word comes to us from (where else?) the KJV, where it appears some thirty times—including a few in the plural form "lovingkindnesses," which is really just too much. The KJV translators picked it up from Miles Coverdale's early sixteenth-century English translation, where it was two words: "loving kindness." Coverdale was translating the Hebrew word חסד, and his two-word phrase is both specific—not just any kindness, but the loving kind, evidently—and also vague: what, in the end, does "loving kindness" actually mean? So we have to go back: what does חסד mean?

Many people today will be familiar with the root of חסד from the word "Hasidic" or "Hasidim," referring to modern ultra-Orthodox individuals, communities, and practices. It would be natural, then, to assume that the word has something to do with piety or adherence to the divine law. In fact, the term goes back to the Talmud, where it refers to those individuals who not only do everything required of them but go above and beyond—also a pretty good definition for the modern ultra-Orthodox.

What's missing from that definition is one of the fundamental aspects of חסד in the Bible. In nearly every one of its more than two hundred attestations, חסד is used relationally: between two people, between a person and a community, and, most often, between God and one or more humans. One does or shows חסד to someone else. What that means in practice may vary, but it is always an expression of favor. Its first occurrence is a fine illustration. Lot, upon being rescued from Sodom, says to the divine beings who have escorted him out of the city, "You have shown me great חסד in saving my life" (Gen 19:19, NRSV).

The most common use of חסד, as noted above, is in reference to God's posture toward Israel. Perhaps its clearest use is in what we might describe as the covenantal language of Deuteronomy 7:9, quoted above, and many similar passages. In the *covenant* between Yahweh and Israel each party must uphold its part. The covenantal obedience that Israel shows Yahweh is denoted by the Hebrew word אהבה, "*love*." The covenantal loyalty that Yahweh shows Israel, in return, is denoted by the word חסד. Thus, as in Deuteronomy 7:9, Yahweh will "keep his covenant and his חסד" for generation upon generation of "those who love (אהב) him and keep his commandments." It is exceptionally rare for the Bible to describe Yahweh as "loving" Israel; it is equally rare for Israel to show חסד toward Yahweh. Though there are of course some exceptions, the general rule holds: these are unidirectional terms, at least in the covenantal context.

We can see the same usage playing out in the human sphere as well. David, after defeating Saul, looks to maintain loyalty to Jonathan, the member of Saul's household who, indeed, "loved" him. He asks, "Is there still anyone left of the house of Saul to whom I may show חסד for Jonathan's sake?" (2 Sam 9:1, NRSV). David later instructs Solomon to do חסד toward the family of Barzillai, who was faithful to David during Absalom's revolt (1 Kgs 2:7). חסד is something that the more powerful party offers to the weaker in exchange for the "*love*" that manifests as obedience.

This covenantal definition of חסד helps explain why it is so often paired in the Bible with the word אמת, often translated as "truth" but far more often meaning "faithfulness." It is not an abstract sense of kindness—it is, rather, the favor that comes from a faithful and loyal fulfillment of one's relational duty to another: "All the paths of Yahweh are חסד and אמת"—loyalty and faithfulness—"for those who keep his covenant and his decrees" (Ps 25:10, NRSV). Loyal obedience is matched with loyal favor.

It is perhaps no wonder that the word חסד is most common in the psalms—over 125 times, more than half of the total for the entire Bible. It is here, of course, that we find the most ardent expressions of both desire for and thanks for divine assistance. These are precisely the contexts in which appeals to and recognition of divine loyalty are most apt. "Let your face shine upon your servant; save me in your חסד," reads Psalm 31:16 (NRSV). "Great is your חסד toward me; you have delivered my soul from the depths of Sheol," says Psalm 86:13 (NRSV).

Since חסד is a quality that the powerful show to the vulnerable, it should be no surprise that it is often taken to mean something like "mercy" (the Hebrew word for which, רחמים, we often find in parallel with חסד: "Answer me, O Yahweh, for your חסד is good; according to your abundant mercy, turn to me," Ps 69:16, NRSV). In these circumstances, the speaker calls upon Yahweh to uphold his end of the covenant, to maintain his loyalty, even though the speaker may have failed to uphold his. "Have mercy upon me, O God, according to your חסד; according to your abundant mercy blot out my transgressions" (Ps 51:1, NRSV).

It's not hard to see how, from this last sense, חסד might have come to be understood as something like "loving kindness." What is requested here is an unwarranted favor, the sort of kindness, we might say, that comes from a preexisting *love*. And, in a way, that isn't so far off, as long as we take "*love*" in its ancient Israelite sense of "covenantal loyalty." חסד is the loyalty, the faithfulness, that is shown by the powerful to those that earn it—and also to those that might fail, sometimes, to deserve it. It is grounded in relationship, and it calls on that relationship as justification for continued favor.

§ 31

Righteousness (צדק, *tzedek*)

And he believed in the Lord; and the Lord reckoned it to him as righteousness.

Genesis 15:6 (NRSV)

"RIGHTEOUSNESS" IS A weighty word. It goes beyond the notion of being merely correct, suggesting the additional layer of being good. It is often paired with "wickedness" as its antonym. It has a strong moral valence and is often associated with a sort of lofty, even divine, justification for one's actions. In the history of language development, big abstract terms like this often have their roots in the more mundane. And so it is with "righteousness."

The Hebrew word צדק (and its female equivalent, צדקה) comes from the legal sphere. In its most basic use, it refers to the party found to be victorious in a trial. Isaiah rails against the corruption of those "who vindicate him who is in the wrong in return for a bribe, and withhold vindication from him who is in the right (צדק)" (Isa 5:23, JPS). The binary in a trial isn't necessarily between "righteous" and "wicked"—often, in ancient Israel as today, court cases are not moral judgments—but, rather, simply between who is adjudged to be "in the right" and who "in the wrong." It is a secondary, and perhaps problematic, development to declare those who win in a court case to be morally righteous and those who lose to be wicked. To put it another way: in court, one side of the case is determined to have merit and the other to be without merit. How easily the legal determination of merit slips into a moral one.

In the Bible, the word צדק nearly always comes up in discourses about judgment, divine or human. From the specific designation of one of the two parties in a court case it comes to be used more abstractly, referring to the practice of deciding a case fairly. Though there is certainly a moral element to being an unbiased judge, it is also eminently practical: "You shall appoint magistrates and officials for your tribes . . . and they shall govern the people with due justice (צדק)" (Deut 16:18, JPS). The next verse defines what this means: "You shall not judge unfairly: you shall show no partiality; you shall not take bribes, for bribes blind the eyes of the discerning and upset the plea of the just (צדיקים)" (16:19, JPS). Similarly: "You shall not render an unfair decision: do not favor the poor or show deference to the rich; judge your kinsman fairly (בצדק)" (Lev 19:15, JPS).

Justice that qualifies as צדק is justice that is fair, that is not swayed by bribes, that decides on the merits of the case and not on the merits, financial or otherwise, of the parties. It is, in other words, equitable—and this is probably better than "righteous" as a way to understand many of the biblical uses of צדק. At the very least, it gives "righteousness" a less abstract meaning. "With righteousness he shall judge the poor" (Isa 11:4, NRSV) is less specific, less grounded, perhaps, than "He shall judge the poor with equity" (Isa 11:4, JPS). One might note that in the NRSV translation the next line of this verse is "and decide with equity for the meek of the earth," thus essentially confirming that "righteousness" and "equity" are conceptually parallel.

The difference between the NRSV and JPS translations of Isaiah 11:4 is typical, if not universal. That is, the Christian translation tends toward the more abstract and perhaps theological rendering, "righteousness," while the Jewish translation leans more toward the practical, "equity." While I am gently suggesting here that the JPS version is closer to the original force of the word, what is perhaps even more important is to recognize that here, as so often, translations are not purely objective, but very much reflect the contexts, religious or otherwise, within which they are produced. Thus, in that most important verse, Genesis 15:6, quoted in the epigraph above, Christian translations from the KJV on have had Yahweh equating Abraham's faith with righteousness, giving it the divine stamp of moral approval in light of Paul's interpretation (Rom 4), that it is faith rather than obedience to the law that is "righteous." The Jewish translation, by contrast, reads, "Because he put his trust in the Lord, he reckoned it to his merit." The JPS rendering still describes divine approval, of course, but with a far more limited scope.

Along with "equity" and "merit" the term צדק can be used to denote "honesty." This is most readily apparent when the word is applied not to humans or to God but to inanimate objects. "You shall have an honest (צדק) balance, honest (צדק) weights" (Lev 19:36, JPS). Morality is off the table here; but equity is very much centered.

It's not a simple term, צדק. Extending out from the party found to be "in the right" in a legal case, it comes to encompass a whole range of related concepts: equity, honesty, merit. These are all aspects of righteousness—they are all good qualities, they are all met with divine approval, they are all worth striving for—but they aren't identical with the abstract and theologically determined notion of righteousness. From exploring and understanding the mundane, tangible, practical background of the term צדק we are reminded that what constitutes righteousness, at least in the Hebrew Bible, is more than just one's inner posture or moral sensibility. It is, rather, how we treat others. It is a sense of fairness, of judging without bias. To do so is both to recognize merit in others and to deserve merit for oneself: "It will be therefore to our merit before the Lord our God to observe faithfully this whole instruction" (Deut 6:25, JPS). Righteousness is not itself the justification; it is the result of acting justly.

§ 32

Ban, Proscription, Devotion, Destruction (חרם, *herem*)

> *"The city and all that is in it shall be devoted to the Lord for destruction."*
>
> Joshua 6:17 (NRSV)

THERE ARE SOME words that we're not sure how to translate: their precise meanings have been lost over time, and we're stuck trying to make a best guess given the context. Then there are words for which the meaning is reasonably clear, but there's simply not a good English equivalent. This word—חרם, variously translated as "the ban" or "the proscription" or "devotion" or "destruction"—is one of those words. It isn't the Hebrew that's hard here, but the English. And it's the stilted English—"the ban"? "proscription"?—that has obscured what's going on in the biblical text.

The basic meaning of חרם is "devote," specifically in the context of devoting objects to Yahweh. Unlike the practice of consecrating objects, in which one can either give the object to the sanctuary or give a cash equivalent (usually plus twenty percent), when an object is "devoted," it must be given to the sanctuary. It becomes instantly and permanently *sacred* and thus irredeemable with money. "Nothing that a person owns that has been made חרם to Yahweh, be it human or animal, or inherited landholding, may be sold or redeemed; every חרם is most holy to

Yahweh" (Lev 27:28, NRSV). In most cases, what this means is that the devoted thing becomes the property of the priests: "Every חרם in Israel shall be yours," Yahweh tells Aaron in Numbers 18:14 (NRSV). But not humans: if a human is "devoted," they must be killed (Lev 27:29).

The rationale for this is rooted in the designation of the "devoted" object as "most holy to Yahweh." Things that are designated as "most holy" have stringent rules attached to their use. *Sacrifices* that are "most holy" must be either consumed on the altar or consumed by the priests. A "most holy" human obviously cannot be consumed by the priests; nor can he serve any other function in the sanctuary, since whoever this poor soul is, he's certainly not a priest, and thus cannot touch any of the *sacred* objects. In all probability, he is a *slave*: after all, the basic category is "that a person owns . . . be it human or animal." With no possible use in the sanctuary, but as a most holy object nonetheless, he is simply killed.

This is all background for the more common and (in)famous use of the term חרם, which is first introduced in Deuteronomy and then becomes a central feature of the story of Israel's conquest of Canaan. In Deuteronomy 7:2 (NRSV), Moses gives specific instructions to Israel to enact after they have conquered the native inhabitants of Canaan: "you must make them חרם. Make no covenant with them and show them no mercy." What this means, in practical terms, is the total and complete destruction of these Canaanite cities. All their inhabitants are to be killed; all of their livestock are to be killed; everything that belongs to them is to be burned. The only things that aren't to be completely destroyed are those that can't be: metals—objects of silver, gold, bronze, and iron—which are to be deposited in the treasury of Yahweh.

As many have observed, this חרם is one of the more ethically troubling aspects of the Bible. Effectively, Yahweh is commanding Israel to engage in genocide, to wipe out, "without mercy," every last breathing

Canaanite, man, woman, and child, as well as all of their possessions, animal or otherwise. For our purposes, it's worth noting that there is a logic at work here that goes beyond mere antagonism toward Canaanites. Deuteronomy, from which this concept of חרם emerges, is clear that though Israel will be engaged in battle with the Canaanites, it is Yahweh who will in fact be defeating them: "The Lord your god will clear away these nations before you" (Deut 7:22, NRSV). What are, under normal circumstances, the spoils of war taken by the victorious army are, in this divine war scenario, spoils belonging to Yahweh. Every bit of them—from human to animal to object—is thus "devoted" to Yahweh.

This is the sin committed by Achan in Joshua 7: "They have taken some of what is חרם—they have stolen" (Jos 7:11). It is not simply that Achan has disobeyed the instruction to destroy everything in Jericho, it is that he has stolen: he has taken objects that belong to Yahweh. This is similarly the sin committed by Saul after he has defeated the Amalekites: he and his troops wiped out all the people but spared the king, Agag, and kept "all that was valuable, and were not willing to utterly destroy (חרם) them; all that was despised and worthless they utterly destroyed (חרם)" (1 Sam 15:9). The spoils—all of them—belong to Yahweh.

From a general idea of "that which is devoted to Yahweh" to the more specific "spoils of a divinely fought war," חרם hasn't changed its core meaning much, just its application. And while the narratives that describe the carrying out of חרם are all set in the distant past, in the conquest of Canaan, there is the possibility of future applications as well. There may not be any Canaanites around anymore, but there are those who are seen by some as unjustly occupying the promised land: Muslims during the Crusades, to take one easy example. And that's taking "promised land" literally—the same חרם notion was also used by Europeans in their colonialist conquest of the Americas, a latter-day "promised land." Even within the Bible itself, Deuteronomy demands that any Israelite who suggests worshipping a different god should, along with his entire household, be treated as חרם. It is not merely a relic of a distant past but a present-day tool of religious enforcement. Those who stray from the path of orthodoxy are, the Bible tells us, essentially Canaanites and deserve the same treatment.

All of this is wrapped up in the word חרם—which is why it is so difficult to translate cleanly and effectively. I will admit that I have long stopped trying to find a good English equivalent, because חרם is an entire constellation of ideas and practices. It entails the killing of humans, the (sometimes sacrificial) killing of animals, the burning of objects, and the seizing of metals. It covers the abstract idea of divine property, of devoting something in its entirety to the sphere of the sacred. It isn't particularly confusing, but it is decidedly complex. A thing is, simply, חרם—and I simply transliterate it, *herem*—and when it is used as a verb, it is always in what is called the causative form, that is, "to make something *herem*." And may the practice always remain as foreign as the term.

§ 33

Grace (חן, *hen*)

But Noah found grace in the eyes of the Lord.

Genesis 6:8 (KJV)

WHEN I TOLD a colleague about this book, and I said, "words that have taken on a different significance to the modern reader than they originally had, for example—" I couldn't even get another word in before he said "grace." Which, to be fair, was also the first word I was going to mention. What makes this such a good example is that it's a word that has a couple of common meanings in English, as well as a very strong and specialized meaning in Christian theology—and none of those quite captures what the underlying Hebrew word, חן, meant a couple of thousand years ago.

Let's set aside common contemporary English uses of "grace." When we see it in our Bibles, it never means "elegance," or "a sense of propriety." No one is going to be "saying grace." At the same time, we should recognize that it would be pretty strange if the Hebrew Bible made mention of the Christian doctrine of grace. That's not to say that there aren't some overlapping features, as we'll see, but we'd be mistaken to read the doctrine of grace into every (or any) use of "grace" in the Bible.

The Christian notion of grace understands it as a feature of the divine: God's unmerited, free gift of assistance (most prominently, though not exclusively, in the form of eternal salvation). In the Hebrew Bible, חן is decidedly something that God can and does give. But, for starters, it is also decidedly not uniquely a divine characteristic. Jacob seeks חן from Esau (Gen 33:8); Joseph gets it from his jailer (Gen 39:4); Saul offers it to David (1 Sam 16:22); David, in turn, seeks it from the Philistine Achish (1 Sam 27:5). And so on. What these, and in fact every occurrence of חן, have in common is that it is given from a superior to a subordinate. No one offers חן to God; it only goes the other way.

The majority of the occurrences of חן come in a fixed phrase: "to find חן in the eyes of" someone, as in the verse about Noah quoted above. Here the Christian idea of grace being unmerited seems to be justified: חן would seem to be entirely in the eye, pun intended, of the beholder. God, or whoever, can decide that someone is worthy of חן or not. Yet most of the time this phrase appears in the Bible, it is not an absolutely groundless appeal but comes along with a rationale. So we read that Noah found חן in the eyes of Yahweh—but we also read in the very next verse that Noah was righteous, blameless in his age (Gen 6:9). That is, Noah deserved חן, above everyone else alive, because he was a better person. When Jacob seeks חן from Esau, he does so by sending gifts and says quite openly that he is trying to gain Esau's חן. David finds חן in the eyes of Saul not for nothing, but because he has soothed Saul's spirit with his lyre playing.

Many modern translations thus render the word as "favor": "if I have found favor in your eyes." Where "favor" works particularly well is in its echoes of royal court language. Supplicants come before the king, seeking royal favors. It is, of course, entirely at the king's discretion as to who will receive those favors—but that discretion is not without reason. Those who have brought gifts are more likely to meet with success; so, too, those who have performed past service or been obedient and loyal: "Yahweh gives חן and glory; he does not withhold goodness from those who act blamelessly" (Ps 84:12); "Turn to me and bestow חן upon me, as is your custom toward those who love your name" (Ps 119:132, NRSV). When Ruth goes to glean in the field, she does so seeking "someone who may show me חן" (Ruth 2:2). And when Boaz does so, she asks him why—because there must be a reason. He tells her, "I have been told of all that you did for your mother-in-law after the death of your husband" (Ruth 2:11, JPS). Ecclesiastes tells us that חן is won by the speech of the wise (Eccl 10:12). The right to bestow חן belongs entirely to the superior party; but there is still a clear sense of deserving or meriting it.

Of course, sometimes the reason one shows kindness to another is somewhat superficial—and sometimes חן comes to signify something, in fact, reasonably close to a contemporary sense of "elegance, beauty." This use is especially prevalent in Proverbs, where the word is used to describe jewelry (Prov 1:9; 4:9), a graceful animal (5:19), or beauty itself (31:30). The prophet Nahum uses the word to describe the seductiveness of a prostitute (Nah 3:4). These are examples of חן that are not bestowed by another at all but are inherent qualities, albeit ones that are perceived by another. "If I have found חן in your eyes" could be translated as "If you find me pleasing." And, indeed, in Deuteronomy 24:1, in the law of divorce, we find the justification for divorce: "A man takes a wife and possesses her. She fails to find חן in his eyes because he finds something obnoxious about her." The NRSV renders this as "she does not please him"; similarly, the JPS reads "she fails to please him." The one who gives חן does so because something about the potential recipient is appealing.

In the end, it's not that the English word "grace" can't be used in these ways. It's rather that the word has become so loaded with other meanings, religious and not, that it's almost too hard to get past them. It's like the word "messiah"—good luck reading that simply as "anointed one" and not hearing all the eschatological connotations that have become attached to it. What חן entails is, indeed, a kindness shown by a superior to an inferior. But it isn't doctrinal, nor is it necessarily undeserved, nor is it the unique power of the deity. We all show חן to others on a regular basis—and we would do well to interrogate our own reasons for doing so. After all, "those who oppress the poor insult their maker, but those who bestow חן on the needy honor him" (Prov 14:21).

§ 34

Sacrifice (זבח, *zevach*; קרבן, *qorban*)

> *The man Elkanah and all his household went up to offer to the Lord the yearly sacrifice.*
>
> 1 Samuel 1:21 (NRSV)

Sacrifice—bloody animal sacrifice—is the defining feature of ancient Israelite religious practice. The slaughter of animals to be offered on the altar was a continuous element of worship from earliest times, both historically and according to the biblical narrative (as in Gen 4:3–4), down to the destruction of the temple in Jerusalem in 70 CE. The practical aspect of sacrifice is thus easily recognizable. Perhaps less clear, obscured by time, language, and interpretation, are both the different types of sacrifices, and the words that are used for them, and in a broader sense what it is that sacrifice was actually meant to accomplish—what it signified.

When we see the word "sacrifice" in our English Bibles, we are usually looking at the translation of the Hebrew word זבח. In some cases, like the verse quoted above, it would seem that this is simply the generic word for "sacrifice." But it isn't. This becomes apparent in other passages, where we find it not by itself, but accompanied by another sacrificial term: for example, "Has the Lord as great delight in burnt offerings and sacrifices (זבח) as in obeying the voice of Yahweh?" (1 Sam 15:22, NRSV). Burnt offerings (עלה)—sometimes known as whole burnt offerings or holocaust offerings—are obviously a type of sacrifice. So it's somewhat strange to see "burnt offerings" used seemingly as an alternative to plain old "sacrifices."

In fact, זבח refers to a specific type of sacrifice. The burnt offering, as is apparent from its name, is consumed entirely on the altar. The זבח, by contrast, is not: Though parts of it (especially the fat) are burned, the smoke going up to Yahweh, much of the sacrificial meat is consumed by humans, divided between the offeror and, as a type of payment, the priests. The זבח is the type of sacrifice offered at festivals, when families would go to the sanctuary to celebrate. It is sometimes known as the "well-being" or "peace" offering. Its full name is זבח שלמים, "sacrifice of well-being," and, somewhat confusingly, it is most often abbreviated one way or the other: either with its second term, שלמים, which is usually translated as "sacrifice of well-being," or with its first, זבח, which, as we have seen, comes out simply, and deceptively, as "sacrifice."

Across the majority of the Bible, these—the burnt offering and the זבח—are the only two types of sacrifices. The sacrifices known as sin offerings or guilt offerings, those that are prescribed in the case of unintentional sin or impurity, are known only within the priestly texts of the Bible: the priestly source of the Pentateuch and Ezekiel. Thus, when we imagine sacrifice in ancient Israel and in most of the Bible, we shouldn't think of it as punitive. Sacrifices were not hardships but mechanisms for communing with the deity, to show appreciation or request help. Think of Abraham building altars as he moved through Canaan; Moses after receiving the law in Exodus 24; Hannah upon giving birth to Samuel in 1 Samuel 1; David when he brought the ark to Jerusalem in 2 Samuel 6; or Solomon when he consecrated the newly built temple in 1 Kings 8.

So much for the different types of sacrifices and what the English word "sacrifice" might signify when we encounter it in the Bible. What remains, then, is to think about what the very idea of "sacrifice" signifies. Here the common use of the term in modern English can be seriously misleading. We tend to use "sacrifice" to mean "giving up something of value." We sacrifice time and energy to various causes: Soldiers sacrifice their lives in battle, baseball players hit sacrifice flies and bunts, giving themselves up to advance the greater cause of the team. It is certainly easy to imagine that sacrifices in ancient Israel were similar: What made an offering to Yahweh meaningful was the giving up of something valuable, the transfer of one's possessions to the deity. What is the worth of an offering, after all, if the one offering it is totally unaffected by the loss?

It is certainly the case that the domestic animals offered as sacrifices in the Bible had value in the agricultural society of ancient Israel, especially for those with lesser means. But there is no indication in the Bible that a sense of loss was part of the conceptual range of sacrifice. Rather, we should return to the root meaning of the English word "sacrifice": to make something *sacred*. Sacrifice, as a ritual act, was most simply the transfer of something non-sacred, or profane, from the human sphere to the divine. Once the animal was designated to be sacrificed, it took on a degree of holiness, such that it could be eaten only by priests or by the offeror (and then only within the general precincts of the sanctuary).

This is the sense of the less frequent term for sacrifice or offering, קרבן. This term, which appears only in the priestly portions of the Bible (and notably in Mark 7:11), comes from the root meaning "to approach, bring close." The verb from the same root is used regularly to denote the bringing of sacrifices. That is, a sacrifice is something that is brought near to God: something that passes from human space to divine space, from human possession to divine possession.

There is some good reason to suspect, with all this in mind, that sacrifice originally was intended as a means of providing sustenance for the deity. The inner room of the sanctuary, after all, is set with a table, bread, wine, and a candelabra for a romantic meal. But there is really no sense of that in the Bible, and I suspect that no ancient Israelite would think that they were feeding Yahweh when they brought their sacrifices. But neither were they engaging in a ritual act that was meant to hurt them, financially or otherwise. Sacrifices, at their core, were like bringing gifts to a king: a way to show gratitude, request protection, provide a reminder of one's existence, and gain access.

§ 35

Redeem (פדה, *p'deh*; גאל, *ga'al*)

> *Remember that you were a slave in Egypt, and the Lord your God redeemed you from there; therefore I command you to do this thing.*
>
> Deuteronomy 24:18 (NRSV)

IN THEOLOGICAL TERMS, redemption is a saving act of God, a rescue from sin or suffering. We are redeemed from what is bad into what is good: from sin to salvation, from death to life. In less theological terms, we redeem coupons and vouchers. No one would talk about rescuing a coupon by redeeming it—in fact, the coupon is discarded when it is redeemed. The two uses of the word seem to have nothing to do with each other. Yet there is no question that, in the Bible at least, theological redemption and what we might term economic redemption are not only related, but, if not identical, then at least conceptually continuous.

There are two Hebrew words that are traditionally translated "redeem." Each has a distinct economic function. One, פדה, is used for the monetary redemption of things that are theoretically destined to be sacrificed. Thus, for example, all firstborn animals are said to belong to Yahweh—or, in practical terms, to the priests. Those animals that can be sacrificed—cattle, sheep, and goats—must be sacrificed. But those that can't—unclean animals and, notably, humans—are to be redeemed. That is, instead of the animal or person going to the priests, their monetary value is donated to the sanctuary instead (Num 18:15–17).

Redemption, in this sense, is a practical matter: The priests are owed what they are owed, and they get it, whether in the flesh or in cash. It is, however, also a matter of life and death: Those lucky creatures that are redeemed are allowed to live; those that are not redeemed are put to death.

The other Hebrew word for "redeem," גאל, is used in cases where ownership of something—or someone—passes hands from one person to another. If an Israelite goes into debt and has to sell his land, one of his kinsmen is obligated to redeem it—that is, to pay to get the land back into the family (Lev 25:25). If the indebted Israelite has to sell himself, to go into debt slavery, he is similarly to be redeemed by a family member, the value of his debt paid off (Lev 25:47–49). In the book of Ruth, these laws are narrativized: When Ruth's husband dies, one of his family members is obligated to purchase his land back from Ruth so that it remains in the clan (Ruth 4:3–4). This is also the same word that is used for the so-called "blood avenger": when one person commits an unsanctioned killing, a member of the slain person's family is permitted to seek vengeance. The "redeemer of blood" seeks, therefore, to recoup the loss of life, blood for blood.

What both words have in common, in their economic uses, is the notion that someone, or something, is being spared: from death via sacrifice, from debt, from falling into the wrong hands. And, as the verse quoted above makes clear, also from slavery, specifically in Egypt. Somewhat remarkably, though perhaps not surprisingly, the redemption from Egypt is described using both of the Hebrew words. In Deuteronomy 24:18 above, it's פדה; in Exodus 6:6, "I will redeem you with an outstretched arm," it's גאל. We might read these as synonyms. Alternatively, we might consider that each emphasizes a different aspect of the Exodus story: the sense of vengeance, maybe, with גאל and the notion of rescue from an otherwise terrible fate with פדה.

But there is also a more practical, even bordering on economic, connotation at play here. Yahweh redeems Israel from Egypt, but this is no pure salvation, no mere change from slavery to freedom. Yahweh makes clear that the reason that Israelites can never be permanent *slaves* to other humans is not because they are forever to be free but because they already have an owner: Yahweh. "To me the people of Israel are slaves; they are my slaves whom I brought out from the land of Egypt" (Lev 25:55). The redemption from Egypt was a transaction: Through the plagues and wonders, Yahweh purchased Israel. Israel wasn't freed—it just changed hands: "O lord Yahweh, do not destroy the people who are your very own possession, whom you redeemed" (Deut 9:26, NRSV). Israel is Yahweh's possession; that is what it means for Yahweh to have redeemed it.

Even without reference to the Exodus story, Yahweh is often described as a redeemer, either of Israel collectively or of an individual. Second Isaiah (the sixth-century prophetic work found in Isaiah 40–55) is particularly fond of this language, which is perhaps not surprising given its context in the post-exilic restoration. In Isaiah, it is always גאל: Israel is imagined to be in a sort of debt-slavery to Babylon, and it is Yahweh who will bring them home. Here, too, however, we find a sense of ownership: "Fear not, for I will redeem you; I have singled you out by name, you are mine" (Isa 43:1, JPS). What's also lurking behind this use of גאל is the notion of kinship: After all, it is the nearest relation who is obligated to redeem. Thus, "You, O Lord, are our father; from of old, your name is 'Our Redeemer'" (Isa 63:16, JPS).

Because redemption, in its economic uses, is always a transition from a bad situation to a better one, it is easily broadened into metaphorical and theological uses: "Redeem me from human oppression, that I may keep your precepts" (Ps 119:134, NRSV). But it is likely that, in ancient Israel at least, no one would have heard even the theologically-charged uses of "redeem" and not understood the various mundane, economic concepts that lie behind it. There are many possible aspects of redemption that could come into play—debt, *sacrifice*, kinship, divine possession, and more—and it is that very variety that makes the term so flexible and useful. It is no mere salvation. It is rooted in the lived experiences of the Israelites and represents both their fears and their deepest desires.

§ 36

Covenant (ברית, *b'rit*)

Now, therefore, if you obey my voice and keep my covenant, you shall be my treasured possession out of all the peoples.

Exodus 19:5 (NRSV)

"COVENANT" IS ONE of those words that, outside of some technical legal settings, most people encounter only as a biblical or religious term. It's got a particular theological heft to it; it's weighty. A covenant is not just an agreement between two parties; it's solemn, it's serious, it's eternal. It's not just a treaty; it's deeper than that, more closely binding. It's not just a promise; it goes beyond mere words—it defines a relationship. The English word "covenant" is weighty. The Hebrew term that it commonly translates, ברית, however, is not. At least, not always. Because in Hebrew, this one word covers "covenant," "agreement," "treaty," and "promise." If not every agreement is a covenant—and we can certainly all agree on that—then not every ברית is a covenant, either. Which means that we have to be careful when we're reading translations that make every occurrence of ברית into something more than it is.

Although we tend to think of a covenant as having some particular importance, the term ברית is often used in the Bible to refer to fairly simple agreements between humans. Abraham and Abimelech make an agreement to basically treat each other fairly (Gen 21:27). Jacob and Laban promise not to harm each other (Gen 31:44). Joshua makes a peace treaty with the Jebusites (Jos 9:15). The inhabitants of Jabesh-gilead make a peace treaty with Nahash the Ammonite (1 Sam 11:1). Solomon and King Hiram of Tyre make a treaty (1 Kgs 5:12). King Asa desires a treaty with Ben-Hadad of Aram (1 Kgs 15:19). And so on. These are hardly moments of high theological meaning (Nahash the Ammonite and the Jabesh-gileadites?). And many translations won't use the word "covenant" for them, but rather "treaty" or even "alliance." But every one of them is a ברית.

"Covenant" is a theological term. But ברית was, or also was, political language. This was the language of the international treaty—and it was that treaty language that the biblical authors adopted to describe Yahweh's agreement with Israel (not the other way around). The treaties that were most prominent in the ancient Near East, especially when the biblical texts were being composed, were suzerain-vassal treaties: agreements made between a dominant power (the suzerain) and a weaker party (the vassal). Though it is perhaps conceptually unfamiliar to us, this is the model for the covenant that Yahweh makes with Israel, especially in Deuteronomy.

The international treaty concept helps to explain why "covenant" is used to describe Israel entering into relationships with other peoples. "Do not make a covenant with the inhabitants of this land" (Judg 2:2, NRSV). Treaties, after all, are exclusive sorts of agreements. If Israel has agreed to be Yahweh's vassal, they can hardly make a parallel treaty with another people or with that people's deities.

The covenant is, fundamentally, the laws that Yahweh imposes on Israel. We hear "covenant" and assume that it has two sides. But when one side has all the power, that's not really what's happening. This covenant is labeled as Yahweh's: "the covenant of Yahweh your god" (Deut 29:12), "his covenant" (Deut 17:2), "my covenant that I have made with them" (Deut 31:16). Perhaps most clearly: "They have transgressed my covenant that I imposed on them" (Jos 7:11, NRSV). And there is never any mention of Yahweh upholding it—it is always and only Israel's responsibility, Israel's failure, Israel's breaking of the covenant (Deut 31:20).

Now, one might say, "Hold on—there's definitely talk in there about Yahweh maintaining his covenant with Israel, too." And that's true. But those verses are never about the covenant made in the wilderness on the basis of the law. Rather, the covenant that Yahweh is regularly said to uphold is a different, much earlier one: "He will not forget the covenant with your ancestors that he swore to them" (Deut 4:31, NRSV). This is the covenant with the patriarchs, back in Genesis. And, though our traditions may tell us otherwise, this too was a one-sided deal—not an imposition of laws to be obeyed by Israel but a unilateral promise from Yahweh without any obligation from Israel.

In Genesis, Yahweh makes three covenants: one with Noah and two with Abraham. They are all promises: to never again bring a flood (Gen 9:11) and to give Abraham land and progeny (Gen 15:18; 17:4). The promise to Abraham is the one that Yahweh remembers when he hears Israel crying out in Egypt (Exod 2:24); it is the one that Yahweh is upholding by bringing Israel into the promised land (Deut 8:18). As an aside: one might ask, isn't circumcision the Israelites' side of the covenant in Genesis 17? Although circumcision is often presented that way, it's not true: Circumcision is a sign of the covenant, not part of the covenant itself, like the rainbow is a sign of the covenant but not the covenant itself.

The "new covenant" of Jeremiah also fits into this pattern. It is, in a sense, a natural development from the two main covenants of Israel's history: the promise to the patriarchs and the laws of the wilderness. As it turned out, those two canceled each other out; Yahweh promised Israel the land, but Israel failed to keep the laws, and so there is, in

Jeremiah's moment, neither land nor obedience. And so Yahweh sets forth a new, third, unilateral covenant: Yahweh will restore and care for Israel, and Israel will obey—but without choice. They will be forced into obedience by the implanting within them of a new heart: "I will put the fear of me in their hearts, so that they may not turn from me" (Jer 32:40, NRSV). This isn't a two-sided agreement; there will be no signing on by Israel. It is a unilateral decree by Yahweh, who is fed up with the disobedient people and their undermining of his plans.

The other major covenant in the Bible is also one-sided: the covenant with David. It is, simply, the promise of eternal kingship, without any named obligation on David's part.

All this is not to say that there aren't any two-sided covenants—there are, some of which we've noted above. Rather, we should simply be reminded that contemporary (often Christian) understandings of "covenant" are not necessarily present in the biblical text, and certainly not every time the word is used. And even when it is a big theological moment—a divine covenant with Abraham, with David, with Israel—it may not be exactly what we've been taught to see.

§ 37

Sabbath (שבת, *shabbat*)

The seventh day is a sabbath to the Lord your God; you shall not do any work.

Exodus 20:10 (NRSV)

IN GOOD EARLY Christian fashion, Augustine argued that, although the rest of the laws of the Hebrew Bible were no longer binding, Christians were indeed still required to follow the Ten Commandments: "Who can say that Christians ought not to be observant to serve the one God with religious obedience, not to worship an idol, not to take the name of the Lord in vain, to honor one's parents, not to commit adulteries, murders, thefts, false witness, not to covet another man's wife, or anything at all that belongs to another man?" One commandment, however, is prominently missing from Augustine's list: the sabbath—the only one of the Ten Commandments that was, and to a large extent remains, specifically Jewish.

In Augustine's time—and for centuries before him and, in fact, down to the present—the sabbath laws, like circumcision and kosher restrictions, were among the most salient and public markers of Jewish identity. It is no wonder that Augustine rebelled against the idea that such a stereotypically Jewish practice should be enshrined in the one set of laws that were still binding on Christians, especially when the rejection of those practices was at the heart of how early Christians sought to separate themselves from their Jewish origins.

Judaism would, of course, come to develop a remarkably thorough set of practices around the sabbath, practices which would come to define both Judaism and the sabbath. But when the Hebrew Bible was written, the sabbath looked nothing like the later Jewish day of rest. It was, somewhat ironically, probably much closer to what would come to be the Christian version of the sabbath.

Despite being featured prominently in the creation account of Genesis 1, the sabbath was not an Israelite innovation. It was borrowed from Mesopotamia, where the *shapattu*, the celebration of the full moon, was, like the commemoration of the new moon at the beginning of each month, a festival occasion. We find the list of "new moon and sabbath and calling of convocation" in Isaiah 1:13. In Isaiah 66:23, "from new moon to new moon and from sabbath to sabbath." Ezekiel 45:17: "the festivals, the new moons, and the sabbaths, all the appointed festivals of the house of Israel." Hosea 2:11: "Her festivals, her new moons, her sabbaths, and all her appointed festivals." And so on. It seems likely that the sabbath began, in Israel as in Mesopotamia, as a monthly celebration of the full moon. It is not entirely clear when it became a weekly occasion, although it was certainly so by the time the priestly text of the Pentateuch, with its explicit link between sabbath and the seventh day of creation, was composed.

To the modern mind (and perhaps especially to the non-Jewish modern mind), there is a stark difference between a festival and the sabbath. One is a day of celebration, the other a day of deprivation. This is, however, a false dichotomy. In the Bible, sabbath observances and festival observances are not nearly so distinct; rather, they inform one another. It is the regulations about the sabbath that give us the model for festivals: Leviticus 23:3 states that on the sabbath "you shall do no work," while on the first and last day of the festival of unleavened bread, too, "you shall not work at your occupations" (Lev 23:7–8). And just as extra *sacrifices* are to be brought on festival days, so too extra *sacrifices* are to be brought on the sabbath (Num 28:9–10). In the two major festival calendars, in Leviticus 23 and Numbers 28–29, sabbath is listed first.

It is useful for our reconception of what the sabbath originally meant to think of it as a festival. There was no festival in ancient Israel without *sacrifice*. Bringing animals to the sanctuary to be slaughtered, staying to receive some of the meat from the sacrifice back from the priests, and then consuming the meat at a celebratory meal was likely an all-day affair. Enforcing a prohibition on work would have been a way to guarantee that no one could prioritize their own economic well-being over the needs of the deity or the sanctuary.

And this is what "work" meant in the context of the sabbath: the means by which one earned a living. The sabbath was, quite simply, not a work day. It was a day set apart—the real meaning of the word usually translated into English as "sanctify" (see *holy*)—for communal ritual obligations.

It would only be with the advent of rabbinic interpretation of the Bible, around the turn of the Common Era, when the "work" prohibited on the sabbath would come to encompass almost every element of human activity, from lighting a fire to carrying an object outside the house. This was the understanding of the sabbath that was known to Augustine and that remains in place for observant Jews to this day. The sabbath in Christianity would, of course, come to be a day for setting aside one's weekday occupation, a day for expanded church rituals, for the Eucharist in particular. It would, in short, come to look more like the sabbath of seventh-century BCE Israel than like the sabbath of contemporary Judaism. Christianity's devaluation of the fourth commandment was, in fact, a response not to the biblical text but to its Jewish interpretation—an interpretation that had totally obscured the original sense of the fourth commandment.

Intermezzo

§ 38

And It Came to Pass (ויהי, *way'hi*)

And it came to pass, as Aaron spake unto the whole congregation of the children of Israel, that they looked toward the wilderness, and, behold, the glory of the Lord appeared in the cloud.

Exodus 16:10 (KJV)

AS SOON AS you encounter the phrase "and it came to pass," you know you're reading or hearing the Bible. Specifically, you're dealing with the King James Version or one of the many translations dependent on it. It's a classic example of what we might call "Bible-ese," a term or turn of phrase that has fallen out of use almost entirely, except in the Bible or in texts that are trying to sound old-fashioned or fancy. What's particularly interesting about this phrase is that, despite it being almost pervasive in the King James—appearing nearly 350 times in the Old Testament—someone reading a more modern translation, such as the NIV or the NRSV, wouldn't see it a single time. What's more, they wouldn't find some current alternative phrase in its place; where it once was, there is now nothing at all. And that's a phenomenon that deserves an explanation.

To understand how the KJV came to render ויהי as "and it came to pass," we need to do a little dive into Hebrew grammar. In brief: what we have here is the verb היה, "to be," conjugated in the third person masculine singular, in the form that is typically used to mark the narrative past. So, to take an early and easy example, we find the exact same word used just as we would use the word "was": "Abel was (ויהי) a keeper of sheep" (Gen 4:2). As you might imagine, this word can just as easily be conjugated in the plural ("The two of them were [ויהיו] naked," Gen 2:25), or the feminine ("Sarai was [ותהי] barren," Gen 11:30). What distinguishes these uses of ויהי from the ones under consideration here, however, is that when used as the normal verb "was/were" there is always a clear subject. Someone or something "was" whatever: a keeper of sheep, naked, barren, etc.

The same word, ויהי, also appears without a subject—and it is in these cases that we find it translated in the KJV as "and it came to pass." It's easy enough to see how the translators got there. After all, they were looking at what looked just like the word "was," but without a subject. So the subject is rendered as the generic "it"—so, "it was." Following the standard practice of translating that *waw* at the beginning of narrative past verbs as the word "and" (see *and*), they got to "and it was." And then they basically fancied it up: "and it came to pass." Now they had a phrase that didn't require a subject, and that could thus stand all by itself in a sentence.

Two other aspects of this translation help fill out the picture. The first is that every time the KJV says "and it came to pass," it comes before a temporal clause, that is, a "when" clause. Starting from the first appearance of the phrase, in Genesis 4:8, the words that follow "and it came to pass" over the next ten occurrences are as follows: "when," "when," "after seven days," "at the end of forty days," "in the six hundredth and first year," "as they journeyed," "when," "when," "in the days of," when," and "when." And so on for the next three hundred-plus citations.

Even in English, then, we can see exactly how the Hebrew uses the word ויהי: always to introduce a temporal clause. And this is, furthermore, why modern translations are able to omit it without any confusion about the meaning of the verse. Look at the quote in the epigraph above from Exodus 16:10. If we take out "and it came to pass" at the beginning, the sentence still makes perfect sense: "As Aaron spake unto the whole congregation of the children of Israel, they looked toward the wilderness." All we have to do is remove the word "that" from "that they looked." And that's easy enough to do, since there is no "that" in the Hebrew—it's been added by the KJV translators to make the sentence work with their "and it came to pass."

What's actually happening in the Hebrew is that ויהי is used in two distinctive ways: one as a normal verb, "was," and one specifically for this purpose, to introduce a temporal clause. What's not immediately apparent to the English reader is that in Biblical Hebrew temporal clauses have no inherent tense, be it past or future. In our verse, for example, the words that follows ויהי mean, literally, "in Aaron's speaking to the whole congregation." The ויהי that precedes the temporal clause is there not to have an independent meaning, "and it came to pass," but rather to tell us, by virtue of its base meaning of "it was," that the temporal clause that follows is to be set in the past. In other words, it's already represented in the KJV translation in the past tense of the verb "spake," which in the Hebrew isn't in the past at all (it's technically an infinitive—a form without tense).

What if the temporal clause was supposed to refer to the future? Well, perhaps unsurprisingly, in those cases Biblical Hebrew puts before the temporal clause not ויהי, "it was," but והיה, "it will be"—which the KJV renders, equally unsurprisingly, as "and it shall come to pass" (see, e.g., Exod 3:21).

The modern translations that seem not to have any equivalent for "and it came to pass" are thus accurately representing the function of the word ויהי in the Hebrew. All they have to do is put the temporal clause in the past tense: "As Aaron spoke to the whole congregation," as the NRSV has it. It's not only better English—it's not Bible-ese—but it also is more like how the sentence would have sounded to an ancient Israelite.

Postscript

§ 39

Bible

I OFFER THIS brief essay as something of a postscript. It differs structurally from all the preceding entries since, as should be apparent, there is no Hebrew term being translated here. In fact, there is no biblical term under discussion here at all. For there is no "Bible" in the Bible.

What we call the collection of books that make up our scriptures is a matter of cultural convention. The term "Bible" was first used around the third century CE to refer to the Christian scriptural canon, in the Greek phrase *ta biblia*, "the books." The use of a common noun here suggests a sort of ontological super-status for these particular books: These are the essential books of this community. The parallel term for the Jewish community works similarly, though it is different: *mikra*, "that which is read," a term in use already in the first two centuries CE.

Even as "Bible" has come to be the standard term, it is somewhat inadequate, or at least insufficiently specific. After all, the Bible for a Jew is different from the Bible for a Christian, and by a pretty wide margin. Even within Christianity, what constitutes "the Bible" isn't consistent from denomination to denomination. We might be better served, if "Bible" is to remain the catchall term, by being more specific: the Catholic Bible, the Protestant Bible, the Greek Orthodox Bible.

When we turn our attention to the scriptures that both Jews and Christians claim, we run into yet another thicket of nomenclature. As noted above, the oldest term for this collection is *mikra*, which is still used within Judaism. The other Jewish name that is sometimes attached to these texts is "Tanakh," an acronym based on the Hebrew names for the three main parts of the collection: Torah (the Pentateuch), Nevi'im (the prophets), and Ketuvim (the writings). This term is specifically Jewish, not only in its use of Hebrew but in the ordering of the materials that it reflects. While Christian Bibles have the prophets at the end (to lead inexorably toward their fulfillment in Jesus), Jewish scriptures end with Chronicles, Ezra, and Nehemiah (in varying order).

The term that is certainly most familiar, of course, is Old Testament. We have been taught, however, at least recently and perhaps mainly in more liberal settings, that "Old Testament" is a problematic term. In its assumption of a New Testament, it suggests a text that has been superseded, that is no longer valid, that is, maybe, passé. It suggests that Judaism, for which of course those texts are the only scripture, is itself superseded, no longer valid, passé. These objections hold weight when the term is used universally, to refer to these books in every context. "Jews read the Old Testament," for example, does feel somewhat wrong. But "for Christians, the Old Testament is the precursor to the New Testament" is quite right, and unproblematic. That is to say, terminology is proper not only to the thing being named but also to the context in which that thing is being used. Jews don't read the Old Testament, but Christians emphatically do—in fact, for the most part they don't read those texts in any other way.

Much modern scholarship, including this book, chooses to employ the term "Hebrew Bible." It's a name invented in modern times by scholars precisely to avoid using "Old Testament." It isn't perfect—after all, there's some Aramaic in the Hebrew Bible—but it does do some important work. In particular, it lifts these texts out of their setting in Christian tradition (and Jewish tradition as well) and treats them instead as works of literature from ancient Israel. It is a means of talking about these texts as they would have been before either Judaism or Christianity existed. But "Hebrew Bible," despite being the term of art in scholarship, has one major flaw: it includes the word "Bible."

What is so hard to remember is that in ancient Israel, when these texts were being written, edited, collected, copied, and read, there was no such thing as the Bible. None of the texts that make up this collection were written for the purpose of being included in it. No one sat down and said, "I think today I'll write something that will go in the Bible." Various texts had authority of different kinds, at different moments, in different places and communities. But there was no concept of a scriptural canon; no notion, I think it safe to say, of "scripture" at all.

The most accurate descriptive phrase for these texts is perhaps something like "the ancient Israelite literary works that would eventually come to have scriptural authority in Judaism and Christianity." It's not quite pithy enough to achieve widespread usage, I'm afraid. But it does recognize that these are texts that in ancient Israel would have been but a small subsection of the extant literature—and they are the texts that have survived and that we attend to as scholars, not on their own merits, so to speak, but because they were included in the scriptural canons of later faith traditions.

Okay, so no one will ever use that phrase. Scholars will continue to say "Hebrew Bible," and Christians will continue, in the context of Christianity please, to say "Old Testament." And Jews will continue to say "Tanakh," as they have for a thousand years or so. But perhaps we should consider the longstanding appeal of both the original Greek term, *ta biblia*, and the original Hebrew term, *mikra*. What is particularly attractive about them is that, as generic nouns, they aren't restrictive. They recognize that what makes these books "the" books, what makes these texts the ones "that are read," is determined, and always has been, by the communities that read, maintain, and transmit them. There is no "Bible" in the Bible. There is "Bible" only in us.

That is, perhaps, the overarching argument of this collection of essays as a whole. Not only the words we use for the Bible but the words that we read in the Bible exist in the space between the text and the reader. What we read in English today is not the same as what was originally written in the Hebrew. The context that we're reading in today isn't the same context that produced the words on the page. What it meant three thousand years ago need not determine what it means for us today. But neither should how we read it today erase entirely what the text once communicated.

The Bible is words—it is, at the end of the day, nothing more than that. How those words have been read and understood has formed the basis of everything from private life to public policy for two thousand years. Yet those words have been inexorably shaped by the cultures in which they have been read and transmitted.

We are the product of millennia of interpretation and translation. But beneath it, still there to be read, and understood, and brought to bear, are the words that serve as windows into a very different world. We still care about that world—it is the world of the Bible, after all, and we're still reading what that world had to say. But we matter, too—we who live in this very different world. What the words of the Bible mean lives between then and now, between there and here, between the text and its readers.